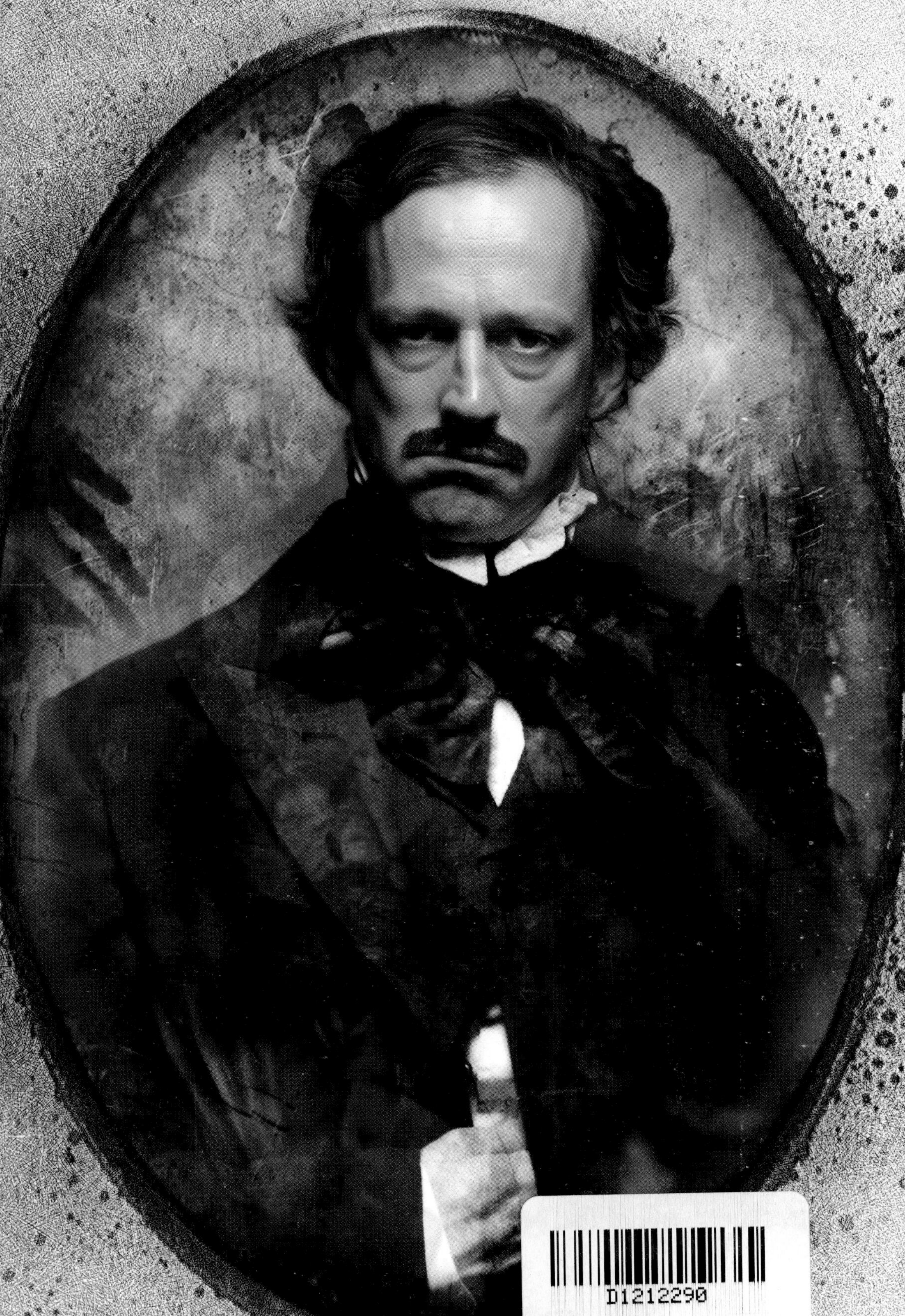

Dedication

Jonathon Scott Fugua
FOR TIM NELSON, A GOOD FRIEND GONE,
who could have, with a few observant
comments and a single entertaining
anecdote from his wild years, shamed
any demon.

Steven Parke
DEDICATED TO TIM NELSON and
E.A.Poe; Baltimore is better for their
company.

Stephen John Phillips
FOR DR. JOHN MILTO IN APPRECIATION
for all he has done for my family.

Jenette Kahn, President & Editor-in-Chief • Paul Levitz, Executive Vice President & Publisher
Karen Berger, VP-Executive Editor • Steve Bunche, Associate Editor
Amie Brockway-Metcalf, Art Director • Georg Brewer, VP-Design & Retail Product Development
Richard Bruning, VP-Creative Director • Patrick Caldon, Senior VP-Finance & Operations
Terri Cunningham, VP-Managing Editor • Dan DiDio, VP-Editorial
Joel Ehrlich, Senior VP-Advertising & Promotions • Alison Gill, VP-Manufacturing
Lillian Laserson, VP & General Counsel • Jim Lee, Editorial Director-WildStorm
David McKillips, VP-Advertising • John Nee, VP-Business Development
Cheryl Rubin, VP-Licensing & Merchandising • Bob Wayne, VP-Sales & Marketing

Cover by Steven Parke and Stephen John Phillips
Cover logo and book design by Steven Parke

Suggested for Mature Readers
Hardcover ISBN 1-56389-928-0
Softcover ISBN 1-4012-0017-6

EDGAR ALLAN POE

Written by Jonathon Scott FUQUA

Digital Illustration by Steven PARKE

Photography by Stephen John PHILLIPS

Lettering by Susan MANGAN

Starring
DAMON NORKO as E.A. Poe
ALICE ADLER as Maria Clemm
HEATHER WALKER as Virginia Clemm-Poe
STEPHEN JOHN PHILLIPS as Sterling Tuttle

...y BY Steven PARKE
& Jonathon Scott FUQUA

This old friend of mine, a board member at Church Home Hospital, which is where Edgar Allan Poe died more than a hundred and fifty years ago, called the journal a hoax.

Still, considering my scholarship, he thought I should see it. He handed it over, looked me in the eye, and I knew he didn't trust me, not even with something he outright dismisses. Am I so far gone?

It was found by a nurse on a shelf in some half-forgotten room on one of the wings that'll be torn down.

My name is Sterling Tuttle, and I'm a scholar at Johns Hopkins University, currently on a forced sabbatical.

If the diary's a fraud, it's an old one, possibly written within weeks of Poe's death. The binding's the right age. Plus, the script's all dripped ink and has the formality and vocabulary of Poe's era.

I turn the page and begin reading.

From the start, I should confess to the urgency with which I write, for I am about to die, this I predict.

Accordingly, the following is a confessional. In short, despite what I have done and the things that I have associated with, I seek salvation from an evil that found sustenance in my soul. The beginnings of my demise can be traced back to 1831, when I was expelled from the United States Military Academy. At the time, penniless and lacking friends, I was adrift and reaching for direction. In due course, I sought stability by returning to the city that would one day warrant unimaginable

I returned to Baltimore.

As before, I took refuge within the alley house of my lovely Aunt Maria Clemm and her eight-year-old daughter, Virginia.

Having published two small pamphlets of poetry, both of which suffered meager sales, I, more than ever, was determined to rise from the ashes of my foster father's renouncements on my character and ambition. I sought to be a writer and scholar of national regard. I sought to prove him wrong.

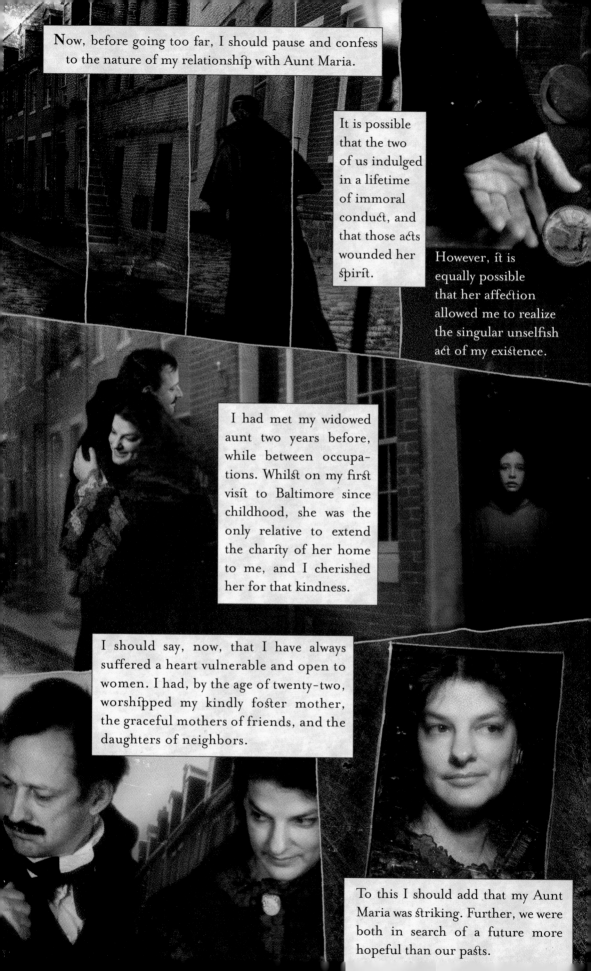

Now, before going too far, I should pause and confess to the nature of my relationship with Aunt Maria.

It is possible that the two of us indulged in a lifetime of immoral conduct, and that those acts wounded her spirit.

However, it is equally possible that her affection allowed me to realize the singular unselfish act of my existence.

I had met my widowed aunt two years before, while between occupations. Whilst on my first visit to Baltimore since childhood, she was the only relative to extend the charity of her home to me, and I cherished her for that kindness.

I should say, now, that I have always suffered a heart vulnerable and open to women. I had, by the age of twenty-two, worshipped my kindly foster mother, the graceful mothers of friends, and the daughters of neighbors.

To this I should add that my Aunt Maria was striking. Further, we were both in search of a future more hopeful than our pasts.

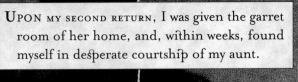

UPON MY SECOND RETURN, I was given the garret room of her home, and, within weeks, found myself in desperate courtship of my aunt.

Further, since the employment of words was my chosen occupation, I used them to great strategy.

Over long months, I broke down Maria's powerful misgivings, drawing her to me with considerate words and thoughtful observations.

From the start, I recognized her as a true gift from God.

And yet, as with many things in my life, even as I achieved, I suffered.

For, as we slowly came to treat each other as partners, I had difficulty submitting to her lover's embrace. In moments preceding physical affection, I experienced obstacles that underscored the burden of our family ties.

"Is this not, in God's eyes, a depraved act, Maria?
Might that be my problem?"

"Edgar, have you
not argued that love
discovered between
two people, whether
strangers or no,
should not be
dismissed?"

"Please, Maria,
do not confront
me with my own
words. Can you see
how I am tortured?
Can you see how
I would have you
if I could?"

"Dear, Edgar."

"I am at a loss. I truly am."

IN THE STIFLING air of my failure, I turned to work. At night, where I had for a short time occupied Maria's scratchy sheets, I wrote madly, searching my soul for stories that would illustrate the complexities of life and the darker sides of humankind. However, working as I was, under false pretense, my creativity ventured astray.

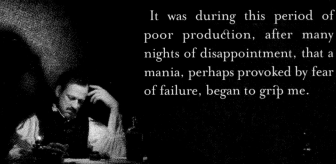

It was during this period of poor production, after many nights of disappointment, that a mania, perhaps provoked by fear of failure, began to grip me.

During one such episode, I came to realize without seeing, without hearing, and without knowing truly, that I was not alone in my garret, that I was being observed.

Intuitively, I knew it was not Maria or Virginia, for they would not disturb my work. Further, I could feel the observer's desire, for it seemed to swell the darkness. Nervous, I commanded the air.

"Who be there? Step into the light!"

"Edgar? Edgar, it is only I."

"And who is I?" I wanted to scream, but dared not.

For in my state of high mania and fitful creation, I was growing unsure of myself. In truth, all of my life I have recognized a close proximity to madness, and on this night I began to presume myself beyond the frontier.

A situation inspired by the fact that I was overworked, guilty for luring then rebuffing Maria, and sleep-deprived for many nights.

"Show yourself, thief."

"I cannot, but I am no thief as you know them to be."

"Who then...?"

"Of course, I am only your father, Edgar. I am what is left of David Poe, the faulty remains of a culpable man, a thing whose desire it is to make amends for his mistakes. I have come to see you succeed where I failed. And with me, I have brought friends to help us find your way."

"My... my father is dead. And if he were not, I do not know him, and he knows not me."

"Edgar, how can you doubt my claim, for I have no greater desire than you. I wish to grant you that which you desire in exchange for my peace."

"We have come in your need, to assuage our hurt."

"If you be my father, show yourself."

"I would, except, as you presumed, I am dead."

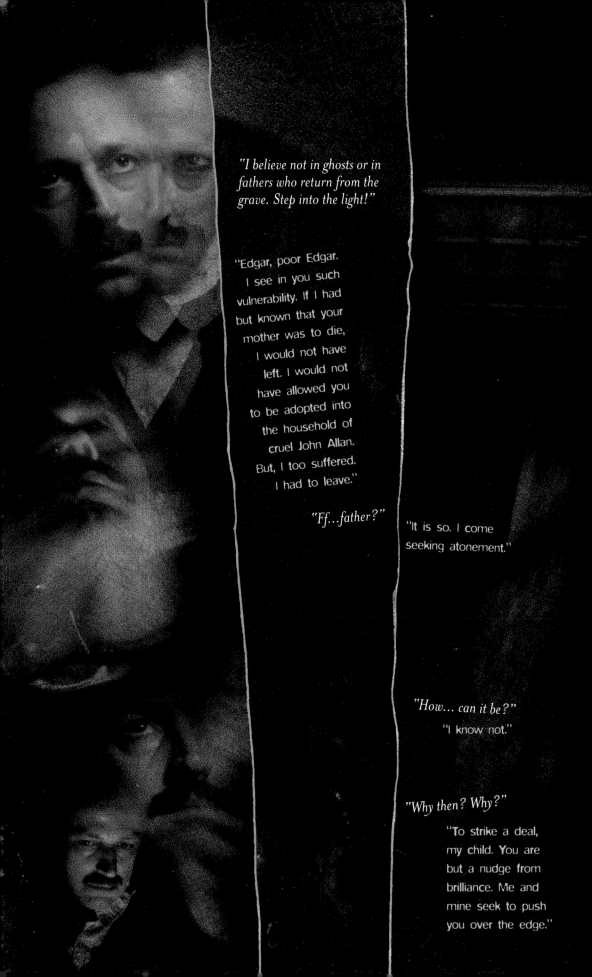

"I believe not in ghosts or in fathers who return from the grave. Step into the light!"

"Edgar, poor Edgar. I see in you such vulnerability. If I had but known that your mother was to die, I would not have left. I would not have allowed you to be adopted into the household of cruel John Allan. But, I too suffered. I had to leave."

"Ff...father?"

"It is so. I come seeking atonement."

"How... can it be?"

"I know not."

"Why then? Why?"

"To strike a deal, my child. You are but a nudge from brilliance. Me and mine seek to push you over the edge."

"I... I have had little luck, father."

"But you will."

"I... I seek fame, but, more, I desire contented love, the former of which, I am shamed to say, I have found. Father, I would have your younger sister, though I know it an unholy thing."

"Edgar, child, when observed beyond the grave, incest is a small, unspectacular sin. It is no shame to entwine the generations. Kings of the Old World enjoyed the company of their siblings."

"I can help you. Do you trust me?"

"I trust my desires."

"Then allow us in."

"Can a wraith inspire a madman? I will merely accept your offer in small form, for I believe you a figment of my mind."

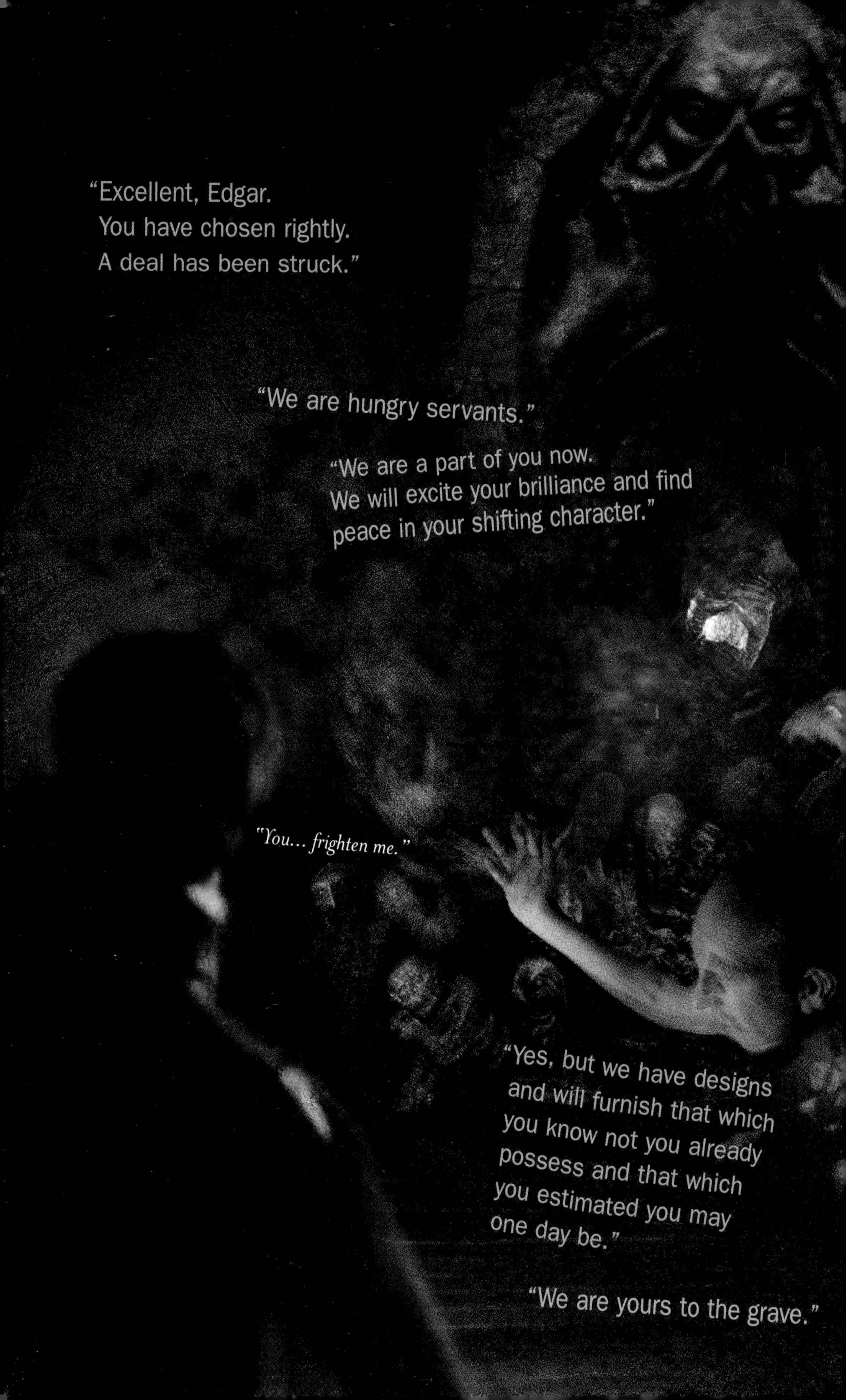
"Excellent, Edgar.
You have chosen rightly.
A deal has been struck."
"We are hungry servants."
"We are a part of you now.
We will excite your brilliance and find
peace in your shifting character."
"You... frighten me."
"Yes, but we have designs
and will furnish that which
you know not you already
possess and that which
you estimated you may
one day be."
"We are yours to the grave."

I *push the diary,* or whatever the hell it is, away. Somebody, shortly after Poe died, wrote this great joke and snared me with it a century and a half later.

As if Poe wasn't insane enough without his dead father and a bunch of demons helping him out.

The fact is, he was a sad, often maddening figure who suffered devastating personal losses.

But his work struck a chord with me once. When I was younger, I came to think I understood him, how he had loved with a wide, weepy sort of heart, how he had cared for his aunt and his wife. Back then I had no notion of grief and how it can destroy.

At any rate, *The Truth: by Edgar A. Poe* might be a forgery, but the writer was correct in that his subject surely had "a heart vulnerable and open to women." I'd argue that it was vulnerable to anyone who showed him kindness.

Loss can make beggars of us all.

I'm alone, teach no classes this semester. At one time, Poe had meant the world to me. I continue reading.

WHETHER ILLUSION OR REALITY, the first months of my father's return filled me with previously unexperienced levels of creativity and amorousness.

During the days, whilst Virginia ran errands, I disturbed Maria's work, her darning of socks and patching of overcoats.

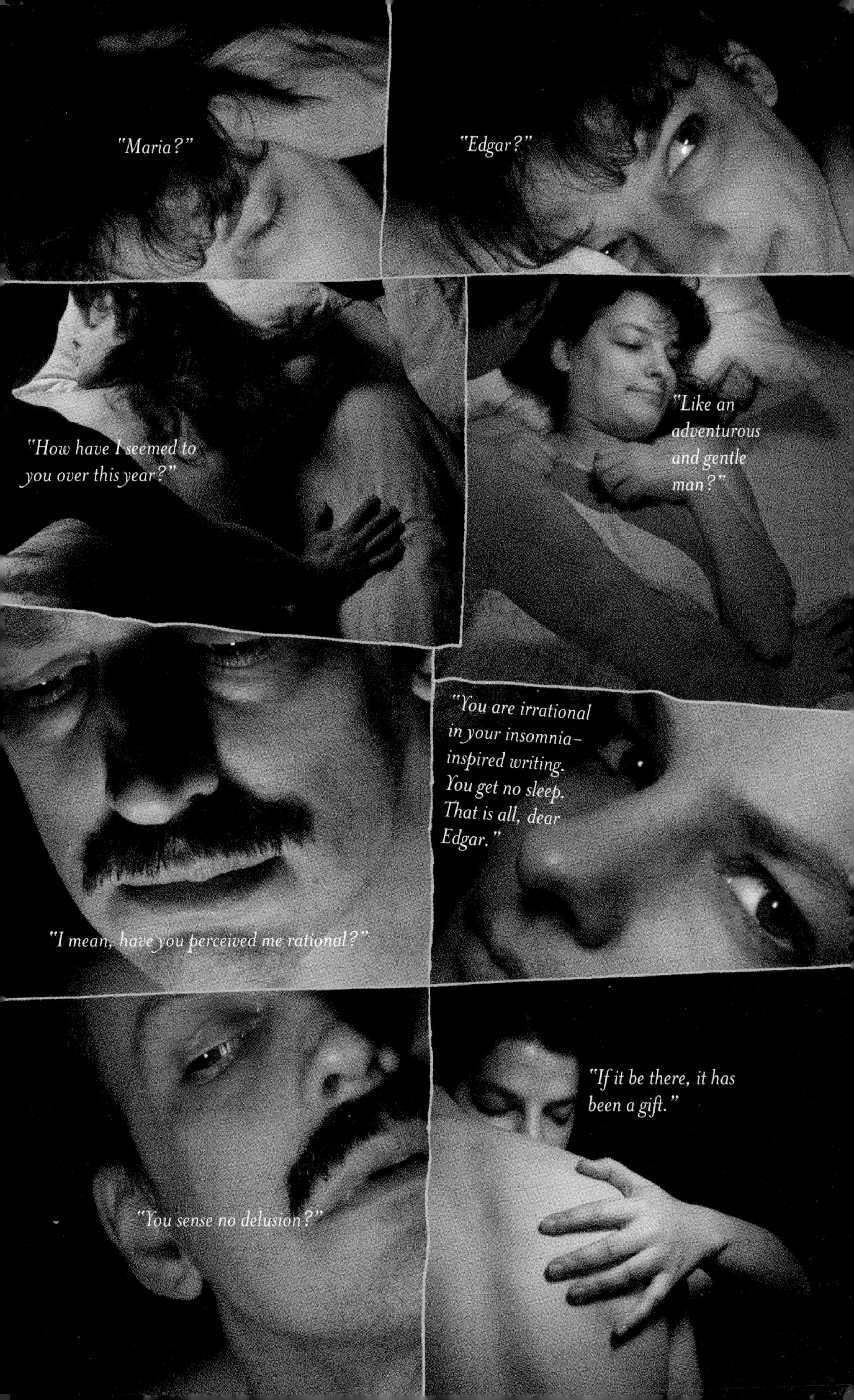
"Maria?"
"Edgar?"
"How have I seemed to you over this year?"
"Like an adventurous and gentle man?"
"I mean, have you perceived me rational?"
"You are irrational in your insomnia-inspired writing. You get no sleep. That is all, dear Edgar."
"You sense no delusion?"
"If it be there, it has been a gift."

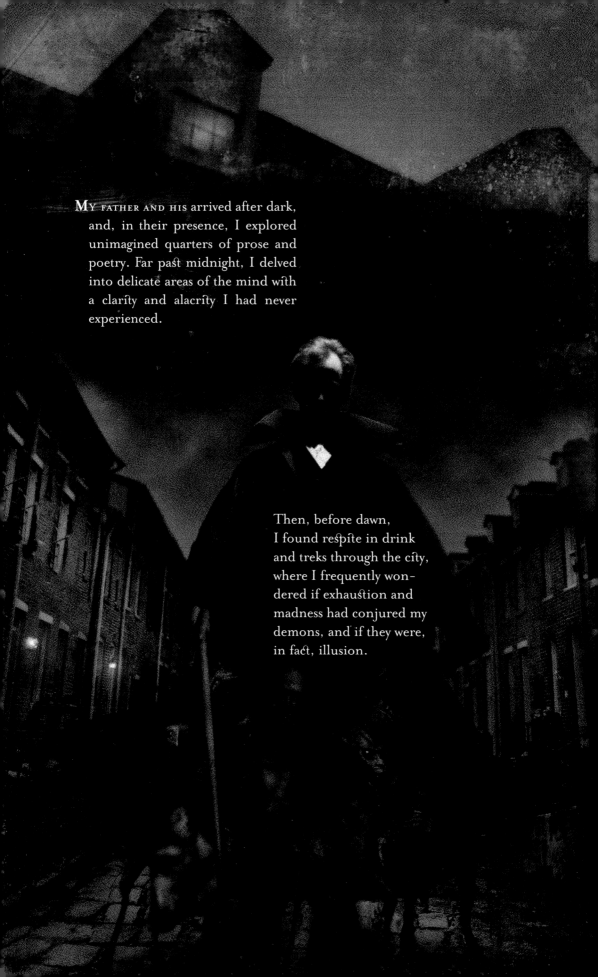

MY FATHER AND HIS arrived after dark, and, in their presence, I explored unimagined quarters of prose and poetry. Far past midnight, I delved into delicate areas of the mind with a clarity and alacrity I had never experienced.

Then, before dawn, I found respite in drink and treks through the city, where I frequently wondered if exhaustion and madness had conjured my demons, and if they were, in fact, illusion.

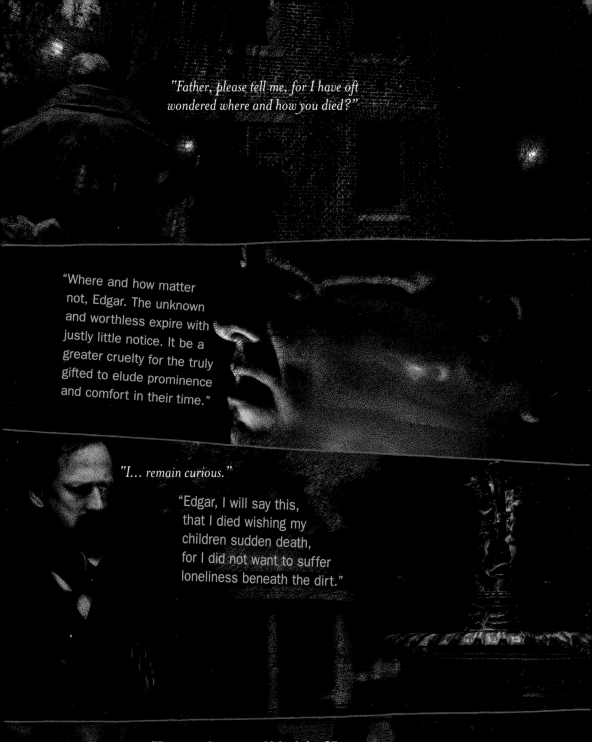

"Father, please tell me, for I have oft wondered where and how you died?"

"Where and how matter not, Edgar. The unknown and worthless expire with justly little notice. It be a greater cruelty for the truly gifted to elude prominence and comfort in their time."

"I... remain curious."

"Edgar, I will say this, that I died wishing my children sudden death, for I did not want to suffer loneliness beneath the dirt."

"Does not that seem selfish, father?"

"And who is more selfish Poe, the forlorn or the incestuous who would have both the mother and the daughter?"

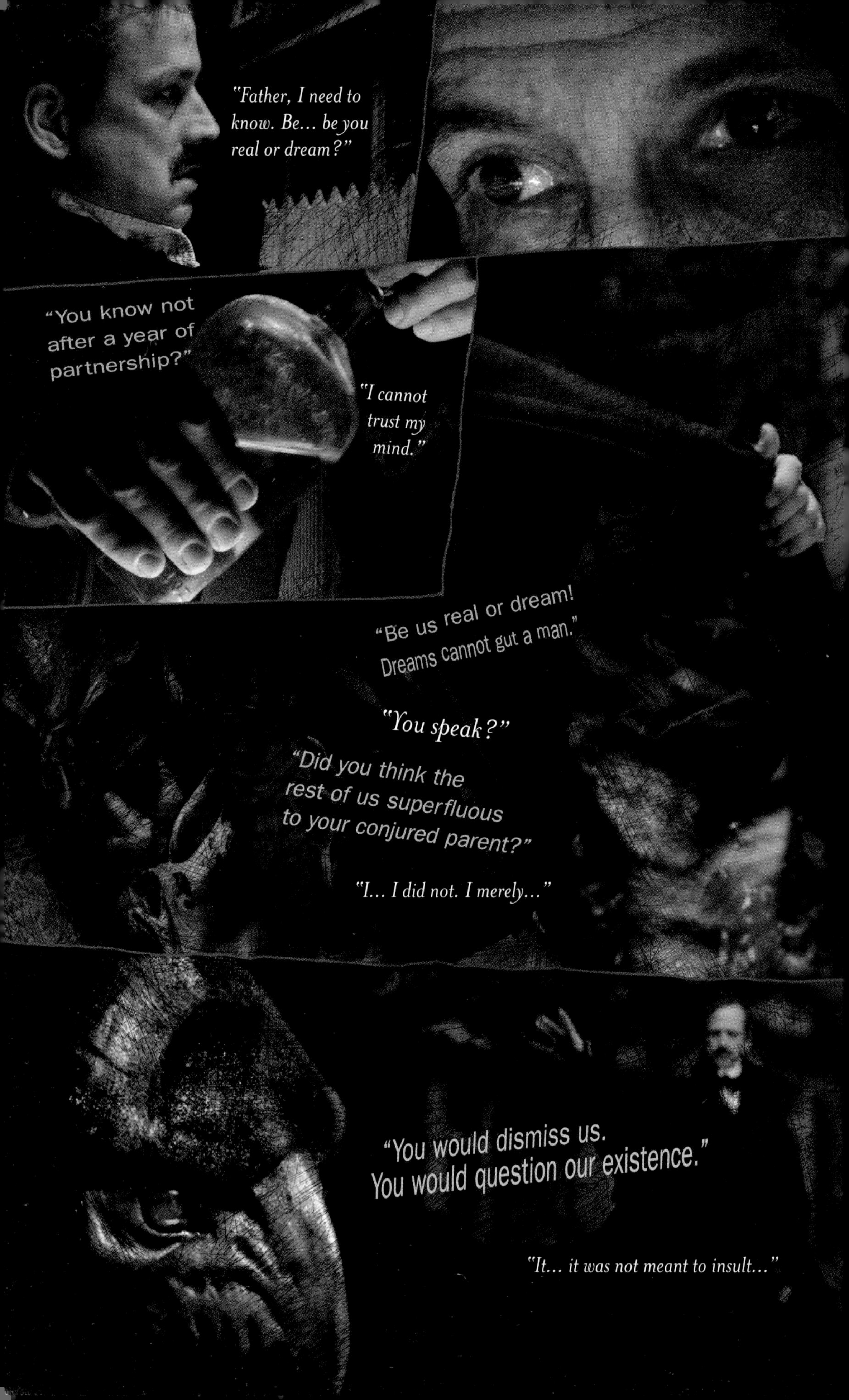

"Father, I need to know. Be... be you real or dream?"
"You know not after a year of partnership?"
"I cannot trust my mind."
"Be us real or dream! Dreams cannot gut a man."
"You speak?"
"Did you think the rest of us superfluous to your conjured parent?"
"I... I did not. I merely..."
"You would dismiss us. You would question our existence."
"It... it was not meant to insult..."

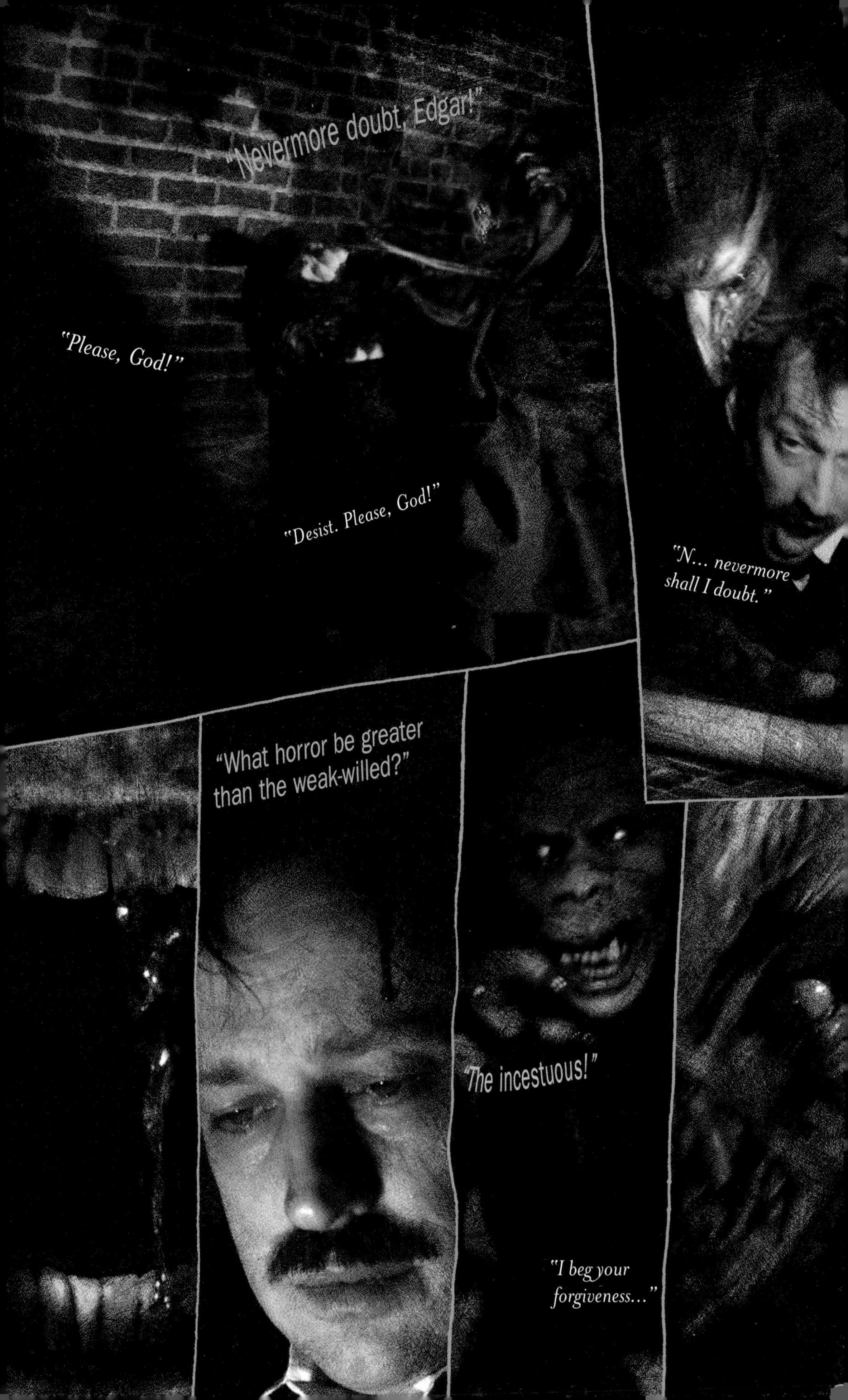
"Nevermore doubt, Edgar!"
"Please, God!"
"Desist. Please, God!"
"N... nevermore shall I doubt."
"What horror be greater than the weak-willed?"
"The incestuous!"
"I beg your forgiveness..."

In the morning,
I told Maria that
I was mugged.

"Poor, Edgar, did your mugger use a hook?"

"I did not see."

After weeks of healing, I continued my work, the nights terrifying but productive. Still, my writings grew darker and more fearful, occupied by vengeance. For months following the attack, I refused to speak to my father, my conjured parent in the phraseology of a demon.

By 1834, however, my career had indeed lurched forward. Stories were published and a prestigious writing contest was won in Baltimore. Though little money saw its way to me, my status grew.

Unfortunately, so did my anguish.

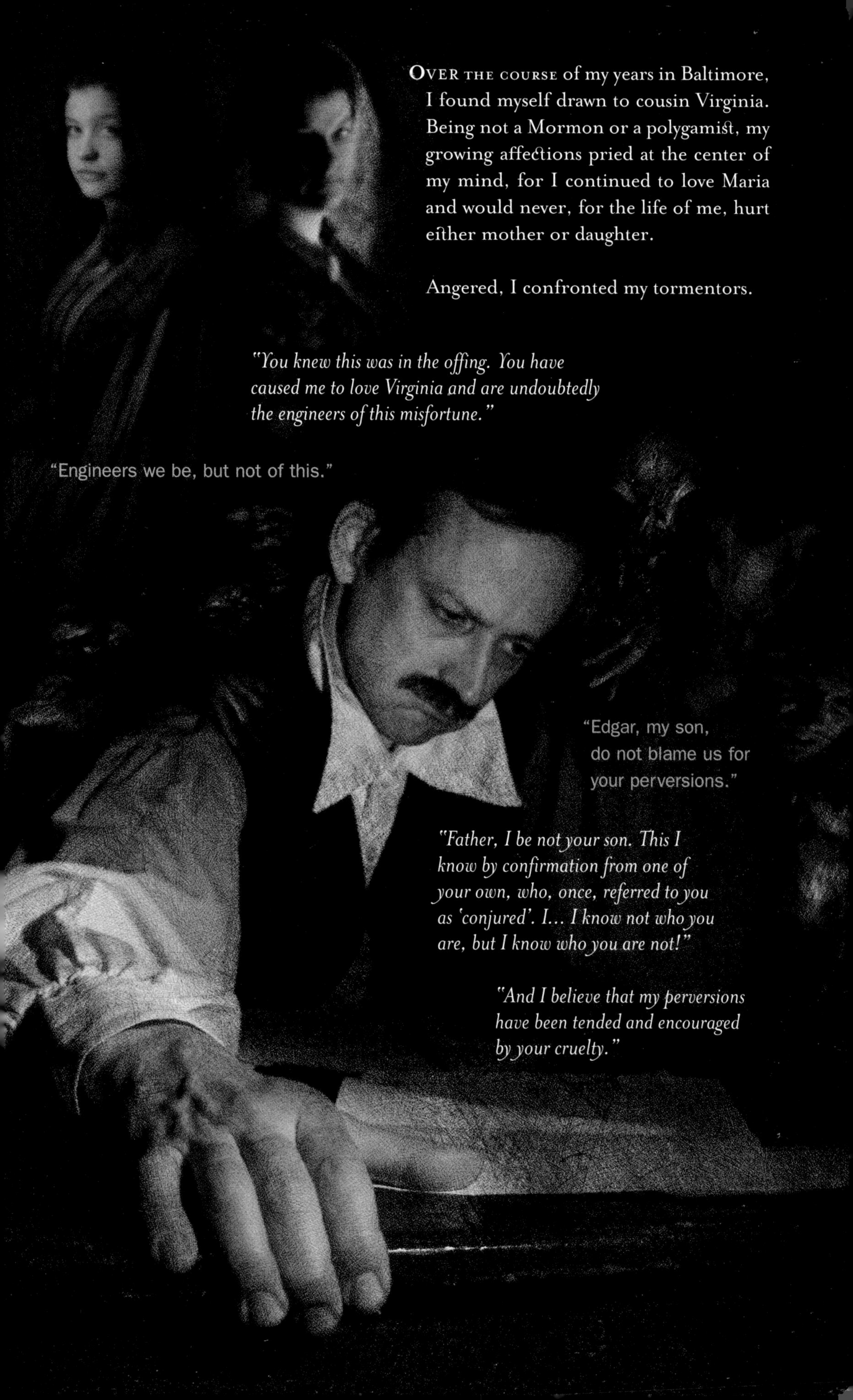

OVER THE COURSE of my years in Baltimore, I found myself drawn to cousin Virginia. Being not a Mormon or a polygamist, my growing affections pried at the center of my mind, for I continued to love Maria and would never, for the life of me, hurt either mother or daughter.

Angered, I confronted my tormentors.

"You knew this was in the offing. You have caused me to love Virginia and are undoubtedly the engineers of this misfortune."

"Engineers we be, but not of this."

"Edgar, my son, do not blame us for your perversions."

"Father, I be not your son. This I know by confirmation from one of your own, who, once, referred to you as 'conjured'. I... I know not who you are, but I know who you are not!"

"And I believe that my perversions have been tended and encouraged by your cruelty."

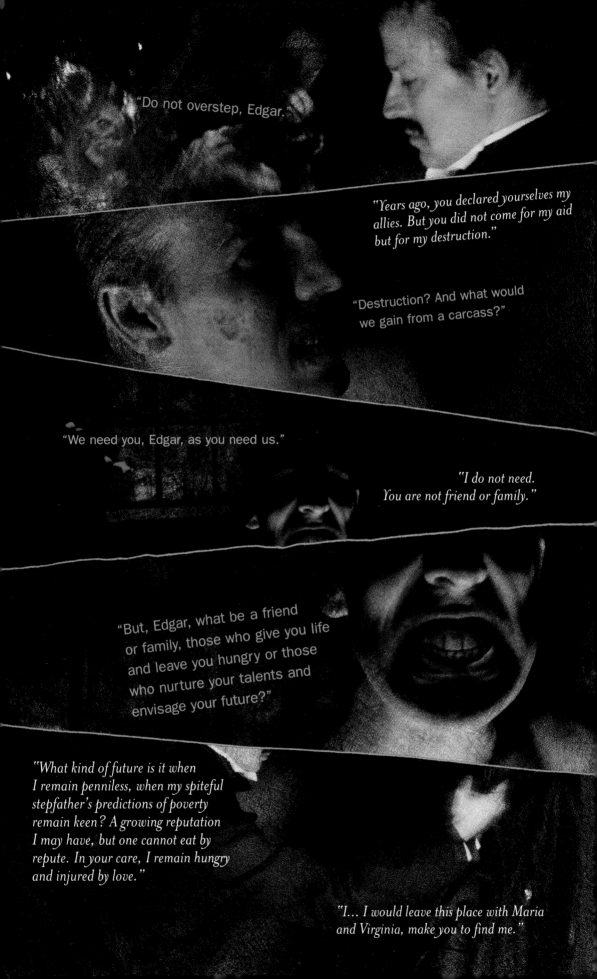

"Do not overstep, Edgar."

"Years ago, you declared yourselves my allies. But you did not come for my aid but for my destruction."

"Destruction? And what would we gain from a carcass?"

"We need you, Edgar, as you need us."

"I do not need. You are not friend or family."

"But, Edgar, what be a friend or family, those who give you life and leave you hungry or those who nurture your talents and envisage your future?"

"What kind of future is it when I remain penniless, when my spiteful stepfather's predictions of poverty remain keen? A growing reputation I may have, but one cannot eat by repute. In your care, I remain hungry and injured by love."

"I... I would leave this place with Maria and Virginia, make you to find me."

"Oh, Edgar, you should go. We are not unfamiliar with escape plans. I admit to you now, we cannot leave this city till your death, but your talents will remain here with us. Without our help, you cannot write. This you should know."

"Consider, too, Edgar, if you stay away, the two you love will suffer. We can dispatch them with ease, manipulate them to be unrecognizable.

On hands and knees, we will force your return."

"Edgar, do not think ill of us. How can we show you the depth of our loyalty? Of course, it is obvious. We will take the life of your stepfather, John Allan. He will haunt you no more. Your wish is granted."

"But... but that was not my wish!"

It was so.

John Allan had died, and I was to blame. My lifelong loathing had delivered a deathblow. My hatred was the source of his demise.

BUT I DID NOT BELIEVE their threats. I did not believe that my skills were commandeered or that they could find me. I would leave Baltimore and take a temporary job in editing. I would obtain a home and hearth in a new city, and call for my two dearests.

We would make better lives.

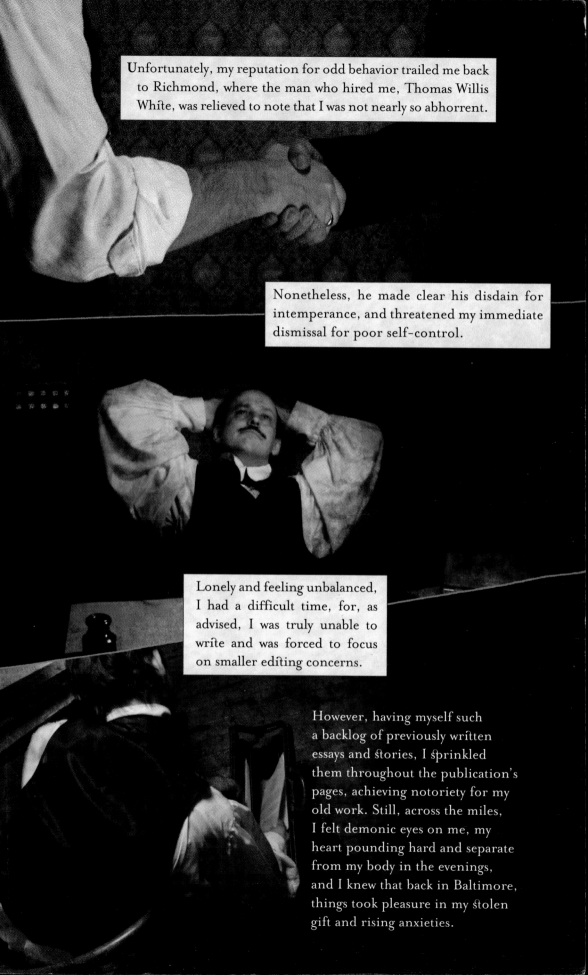

Unfortunately, my reputation for odd behavior trailed me back to Richmond, where the man who hired me, Thomas Willis White, was relieved to note that I was not nearly so abhorrent.

Nonetheless, he made clear his disdain for intemperance, and threatened my immediate dismissal for poor self-control.

Lonely and feeling unbalanced, I had a difficult time, for, as advised, I was truly unable to write and was forced to focus on smaller editing concerns.

However, having myself such a backlog of previously written essays and stories, I sprinkled them throughout the publication's pages, achieving notoriety for my old work. Still, across the miles, I felt demonic eyes on me, my heart pounding hard and separate from my body in the evenings, and I knew that back in Baltimore, things took pleasure in my stolen gift and rising anxieties.

At the very soonest
moment possible,
I found rooms in
a tattered boarding
house and sent for
Maria and Virginia.

Days later, a letter arrived.

Dear Edgar,

It is with heavy heart that I admit to questioning the
intelligence of a move to Richmond. It seems that at
every corner, we are beseeched by others to stay in
Baltimore. Further, your Uncle Neilson has insisted
us to be permanent houseguests at his residence.
I must admit to you that I believe he has done so in
an unnecessary attempt to keep Virginia from
marrying you, as is rumored your want in our
small circles. Though I have plainly explained to him that
she is not of your interest, he seems categorically
certain that you would wed her if given the chance.
Please advise me in this difficult time.

With all of my love,

Maria

In Maria's
communication,
I recognized the
influence of my
tormentors, for
nobody but they
would guess my
matrimonial
intentions.

Angry, I took quill to paper in
a form that still begets self-disgust,
for I was suddenly aware that, should
they follow me, Maria and Virginia's
lives would be at risk.

I am not a noble man. To Maria, I hid the shabby nature of my lodgings and concealed the truth about my love for cousin Virginia. I denied them both a chance for a better life wih Neilson Poe.

Dear Maria,

I am blinded by tears while writing this letter. My last my only hold on life is cruelly torn away. I love, you know I love you and Virginia devotedly. I cannot express in words the fervent devotion I feel towards my dear aunt and little cousin - my own darlings. All my thoughts are occupied with the supposition that both of you would prefer to go with Neilson Poe.

I admit that I love cousin Virginia, but it means not that I love you less for it, for love can come in different forms. I would have you both with me, for she is in need of adults. I would take you as my wife if social morays permitted. Pity me, my dear Auntie, pity me. I have no one now to fly to - I am among strangers.

Sadly, I have already procured a sweet little house for you both It is in a retired situation on Church Hill - newly done up and with every convenience. What is the use? The tone of your letter wounds me to the soul. My darling love, my own sweetest Auntie, think well before you break my heart.

Edgar

IN RETROSPECT, my correspondence was a pitiful, martyr's ploy to draw out sympathy and emotion and bury considered thought.

Oh, that Maria had run the other way. If so, Virginia might now be alive.

In consideration of my past, though, how could I have responded differently? As a child, I lost both parents and grew fearful of solitude.

I could not endure it long, for, in it, I sensed the Angel of Death's terrifying closeness. As a boy, I had sought to write away these fears by placing them on paper.

In fact, story creation had been my single unshakeable companion, and, now, it too had forsaken me.

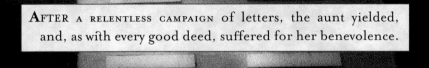

AFTER A RELENTLESS CAMPAIGN of letters, the aunt yielded, and, as with every good deed, suffered for her benevolence.

In Richmond, Maria had no work whilst Virginia was frightened by the smallness of the city and largeness of our boarding home.

But, I told myself, we were family, and I needed them to help allay my misery and set aside my past. So, every night, I carried home gifts for them both, wildflowers, bird nests, hard candy, and pretty scraps of fabric or paper. All were received with graciousness, which is exactly what I felt in the giving.

During lunchtime hours, one or the other would meet me. Hand in hand, we would stroll the cool streets of the state capital, love enshrouding.

"Virginia, speak truth to me. Are you acclimating to this city?"

"It is stranger than Baltimore, Uncle, the people unnerving. But... because you are happy, I will survive."

"Would my contentment truly give you strength?"

"Kindness should see reward."

"Oh, Virginia, at times it does. It does in your presence and the presence of your dear mother. Poor and unknown I would accept of my life if I could love you both."

"Must we be poor, Uncle? Can we aspire to riches? Momma says you will be famous."

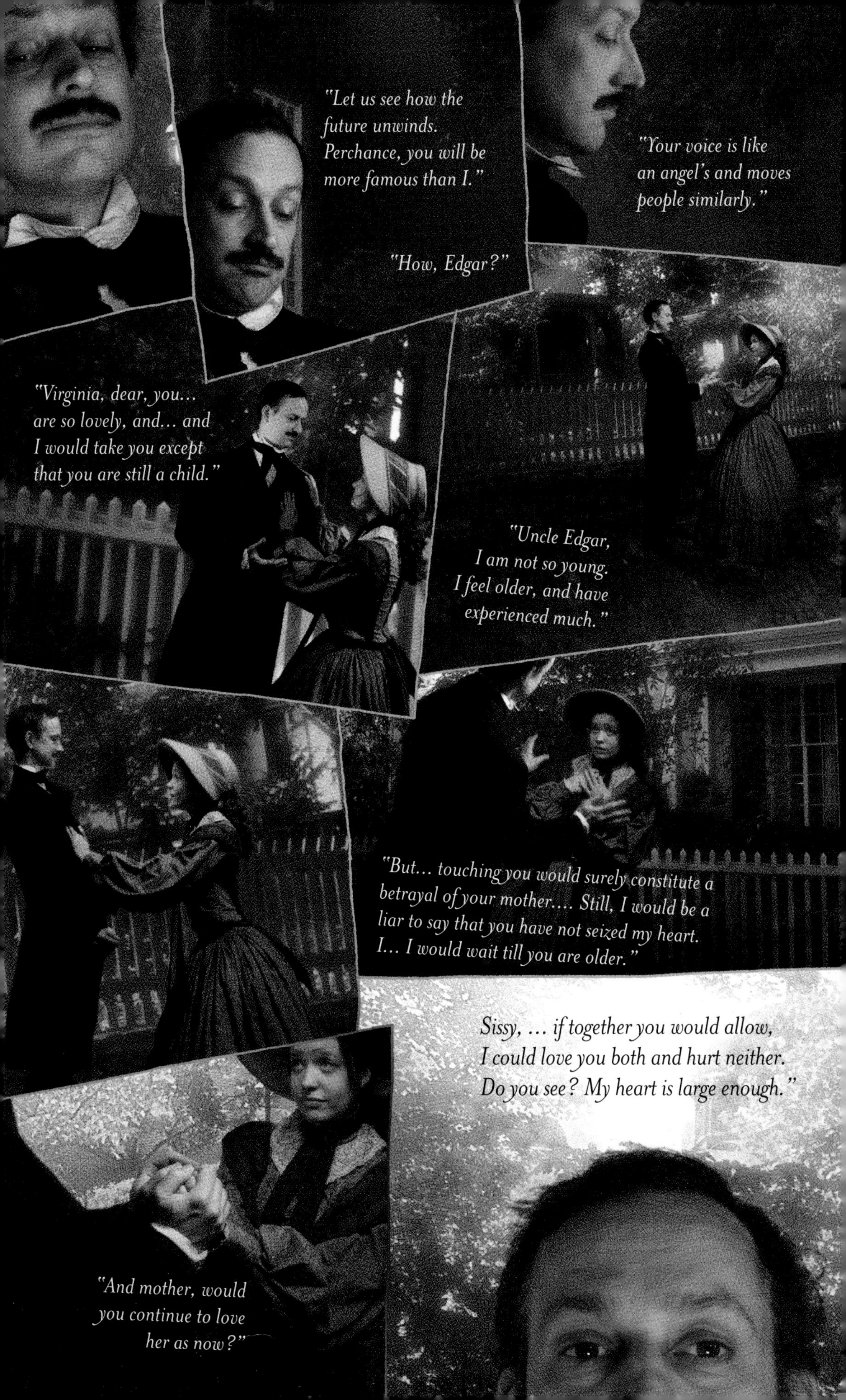
"Let us see how the future unwinds. Perchance, you will be more famous than I."
"How, Edgar?"
"Your voice is like an angel's and moves people similarly."
"Virginia, dear, you... are so lovely, and... and I would take you except that you are still a child."
"Uncle Edgar, I am not so young. I feel older, and have experienced much."
"But... touching you would surely constitute a betrayal of your mother.... Still, I would be a liar to say that you have not seized my heart. I... I would wait till you are older."
"And mother, would you continue to love her as now?"
Sissy, ... if together you would allow, I could love you both and hurt neither. Do you see? My heart is large enough."

"I know your thoughts. Certainly, it makes for a curious family, but, for people like us, tradition need not be heeded."

"Artists live outside the mainstream. People will allow it."

At work, the months passed, and my writing frustrations and vague but escalating fears bore holes through my innards and unbalanced my mind.

Simultaneously, my literary reputation swelled, for I was publishing old work monthly even though I could barely pen correspondence for the magazine.

"I have lost my talent! Things watch me. I sense them growing desperate. They... they have stolen my art form and attempt to frighten me."

"Edgar, you suffer a lack of confidence, nothing more. It seems evident in your growing fears of darkness."

"No, it is more. I am cursed. I am being mined for my instability."

"But, Edgar, 'The Messenger' has thrived in your care, and your writings have been praised."

"Thrived. Maria, the magazine travels by its own momentum. Please, on this subject, I cannot stand to hear falsehoods. I beg you not to convince me otherwise."

"I would help, that is all."

"Help? Few of flesh and blood can. I... I find so little peace these days. There are but two sources in my life. Two."

"Then say to me those sources, Edgar, and I will supply them with greater consistency."

"You... you could not. For they would cause great pain."

"Great pain I would endure."

"It is you and Virginia. What I at first denied has come to unbearable passage. I... I believe I had no control in the matter, but in these few months... I have fallen in love with my cousin... I would this minute marry her, but...

Maria, I would still have you. One and two are the source and strength of my joys. I need both."

"How could you give me so much? It would be a grand act of altruism. How could you allow me to show the largeness of my heart?"

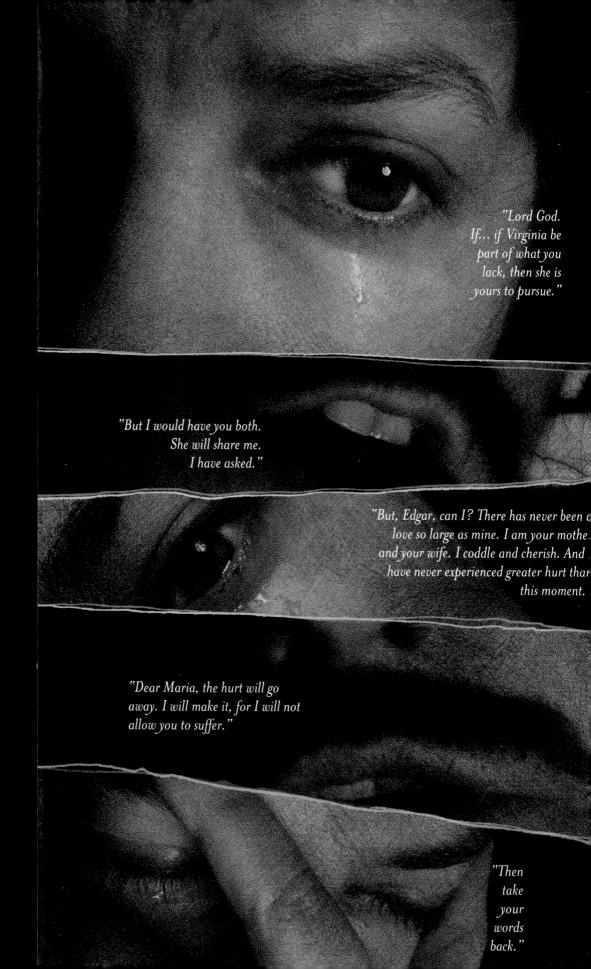

"Lord God.
If... if Virginia be
part of what you
lack, then she is
yours to pursue."

"But I would have you both.
She will share me.
I have asked."

"But, Edgar, can I? There has never been [c]
love so large as mine. I am your mothe[r]
and your wife. I coddle and cherish. And [I]
have never experienced greater hurt tha[n]
this moment.[?]

"Dear Maria, the hurt will go
away. I will make it, for I will not
allow you to suffer."

"Then
take
your
words
back."

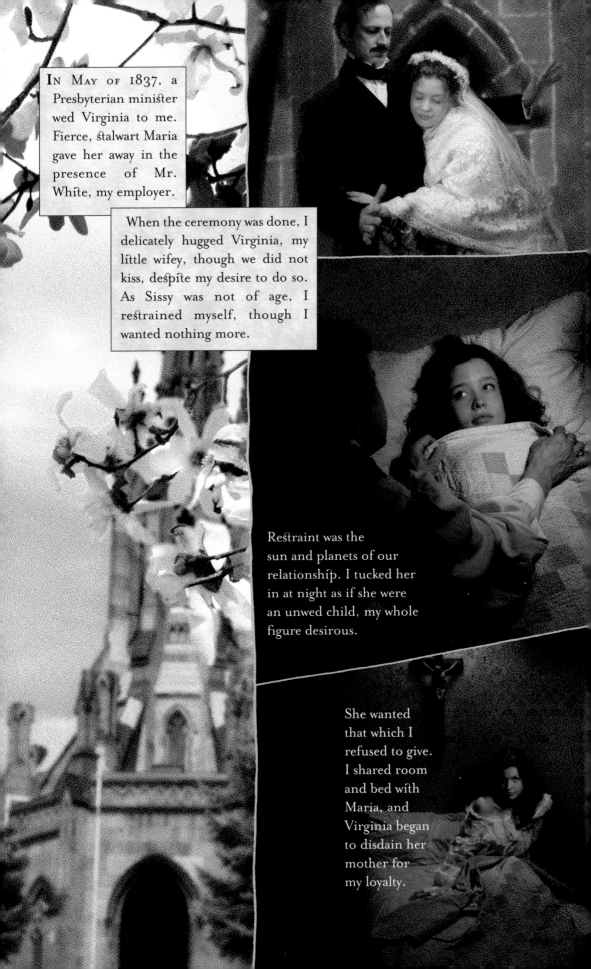

IN MAY OF 1837, a Presbyterian minister wed Virginia to me. Fierce, stalwart Maria gave her away in the presence of Mr. White, my employer.

When the ceremony was done, I delicately hugged Virginia, my little wifey, though we did not kiss, despite my desire to do so. As Sissy was not of age, I restrained myself, though I wanted nothing more.

Restraint was the sun and planets of our relationship. I tucked her in at night as if she were an unwed child, my whole figure desirous.

She wanted that which I refused to give. I shared room and bed with Maria, and Virginia began to disdain her mother for my loyalty.

I *ponder* what I've just read, confused by the words and considering the unfeasible.

If my mind wasn't quite so cloudy, I would know, as I once did, the exact dates of Poe's travels, marriage and when he published.

But I've been drinking and need to look both up in order to corroborate what I suspect to be disturbingly accurate.

I study Poe's near-mad looking image, and I'm shaken by the torment in his eyes.

THE SOUTHERN LITERARY MESSENGER'S claustrophobic offices came to throb painfully in my chest, to take pleasure in my inability to produce. I would not have been surprised to see my grotesque demons tumble mockingly from the shadows of my desk.

Further, in the course of a few years, I used up all of my old work and anxiously disguised my lack of production behind farcical editorial duties, mounds of paper, and reprises.

Thus stressed and unhappy, of course I drank. In such time, after nearly two years, my demons called on me in Richmond.

"Edgar. Edgar."

"Who... who speaks?"

"Edgar. It is time."

"No, you were but illusions of an unwell mind."

"Illusions cannot commit murder or leave scars."

"Lea... leave me! Leave me to my uselessness! You said you could not follow."

"Impatient from hunger, We would force your hand."

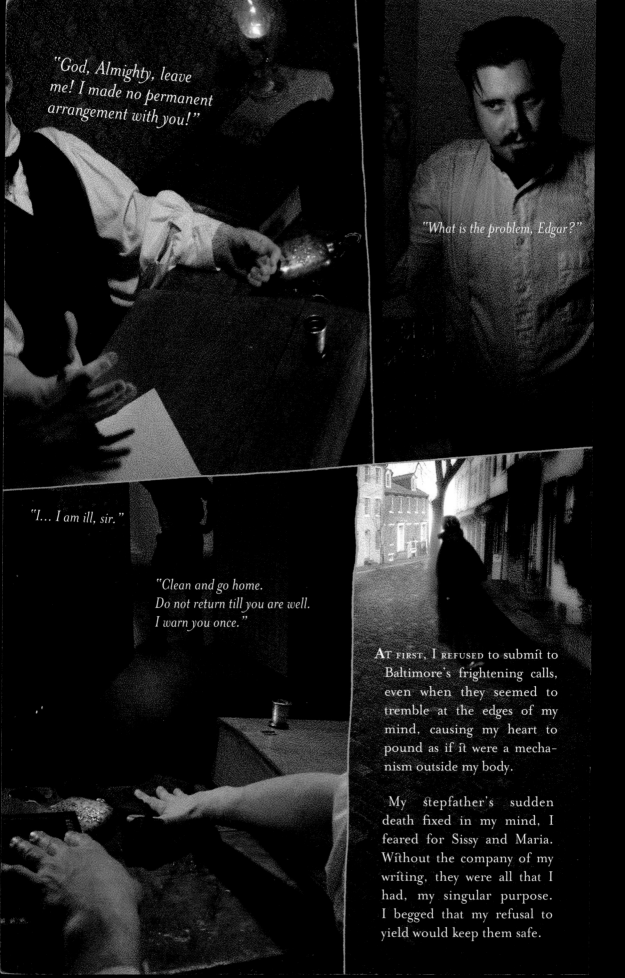

"God, Almighty, leave me! I made no permanent arrangement with you!"

"What is the problem, Edgar?"

"I... I am ill, sir."

"Clean and go home. Do not return till you are well. I warn you once."

AT FIRST, I REFUSED to submit to Baltimore's frightening calls, even when they seemed to tremble at the edges of my mind, causing my heart to pound as if it were a mechanism outside my body.

My stepfather's sudden death fixed in my mind, I feared for Sissy and Maria. Without the company of my writing, they were all that I had, my singular purpose. I begged that my refusal to yield would keep them safe.

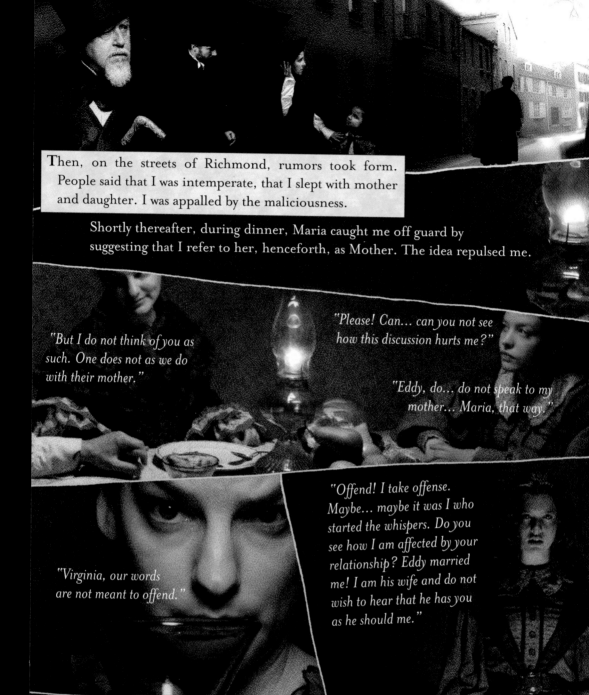

Then, on the streets of Richmond, rumors took form. People said that I was intemperate, that I slept with mother and daughter. I was appalled by the maliciousness.

Shortly thereafter, during dinner, Maria caught me off guard by suggesting that I refer to her, henceforth, as Mother. The idea repulsed me.

"Please! Can... can you not see how this discussion hurts me?"

"But I do not think of you as such. One does not as we do with their mother."

"Eddy, do... do not speak to my mother... Maria, that way."

"Offend! I take offense. Maybe... maybe it was I who started the whispers. Do you see how I am affected by your relationship? Eddy married me! I am his wife and do not wish to hear that he has you as he should me."

"Virginia, our words are not meant to offend."

"I... I married you both."

"Virginia, stop!"

"Live your lies! Live them, and I will live my own."

"Sissy, please."

"Virginia, I do love
you. But you are still
young. The time for us
is coming."

"If you love me,
do so outright."

"Sissy, I have given
my dreams for you
and your mother.
These years... they
have been misery."

"I am tortured,
a tortured man."

"I would
return to my
own work but
for you both,
whom I care
for as no one
has cared
for two."

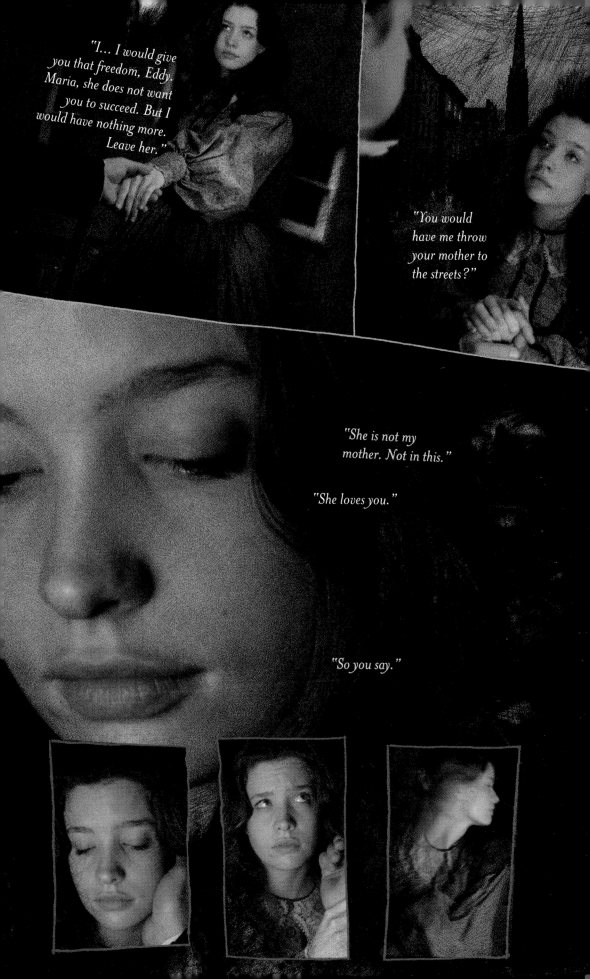

"I... I would give you that freedom, Eddy. Maria, she does not want you to succeed. But I would have nothing more. Leave her."

"You would have me throw your mother to the streets?"

"She is not my mother. Not in this."

"She loves you."

"So you say."

"Maria! Speak to me."

"I have been attacked, Edgar! I went out looking for you and Virginia, and I was robbed! A man, enormous and shabbily dressed, rushed from the shadows and knocked me to my knees."

"He... he said to me, 'We are calling Him home.' He said 'We are calling him home and would kill you in his refusal.' He tore my bag from my grip. I... I don't understand. Did he mean you?"

"No."

"I think he did. I think he did, Edgar."

A WEEK LATER, on the pretext of scouting publishers in New York and Philadelphia, I took short-term leave at *The Messenger*, traveled northward and away from Sissy and Mother.

Of course, I, instead, returned to vile Baltimore.

During daylight hours, I obtained short-term board in a whorehouse and, frightened, waited for night, terrified by what I might see whilst simultaneously fearful that my mind had fabricated all.

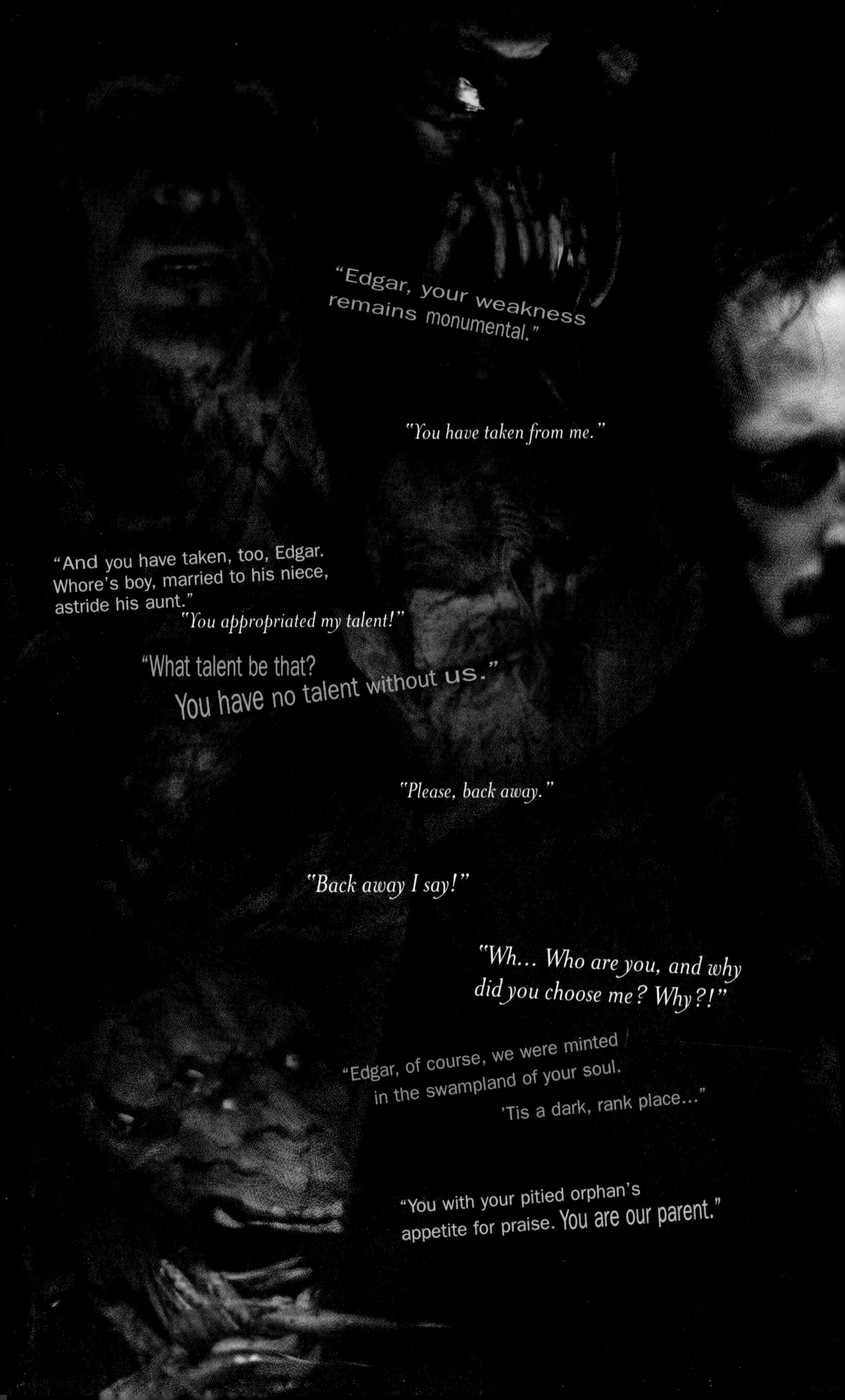
"Edgar, your weakness remains monumental."
"You have taken from me."
"And you have taken, too, Edgar. Whore's boy, married to his niece, astride his aunt."
"You appropriated my talent!"
"What talent be that? You have no talent without us."
"Please, back away."
"Back away I say!"
"Wh... Who are you, and why did you choose me? Why?!"
"Edgar, of course, we were minted in the swampland of your soul. 'Tis a dark, rank place..."
"You with your pitied orphan's appetite for praise. You are our parent."

"You steal, manipulate, and seek to control! You threatened Mother's death to draw me back. You are no child of mine."

"We did not touch your aging Mother, for we knew you would return."

"Liars. In this I cannot abide falsehood. I... I know a blade's use from my days in the military. You may murder me, but I will cut you in horrible ways."

"Edgar, we would not hurt Maria. It is only you that we desire."

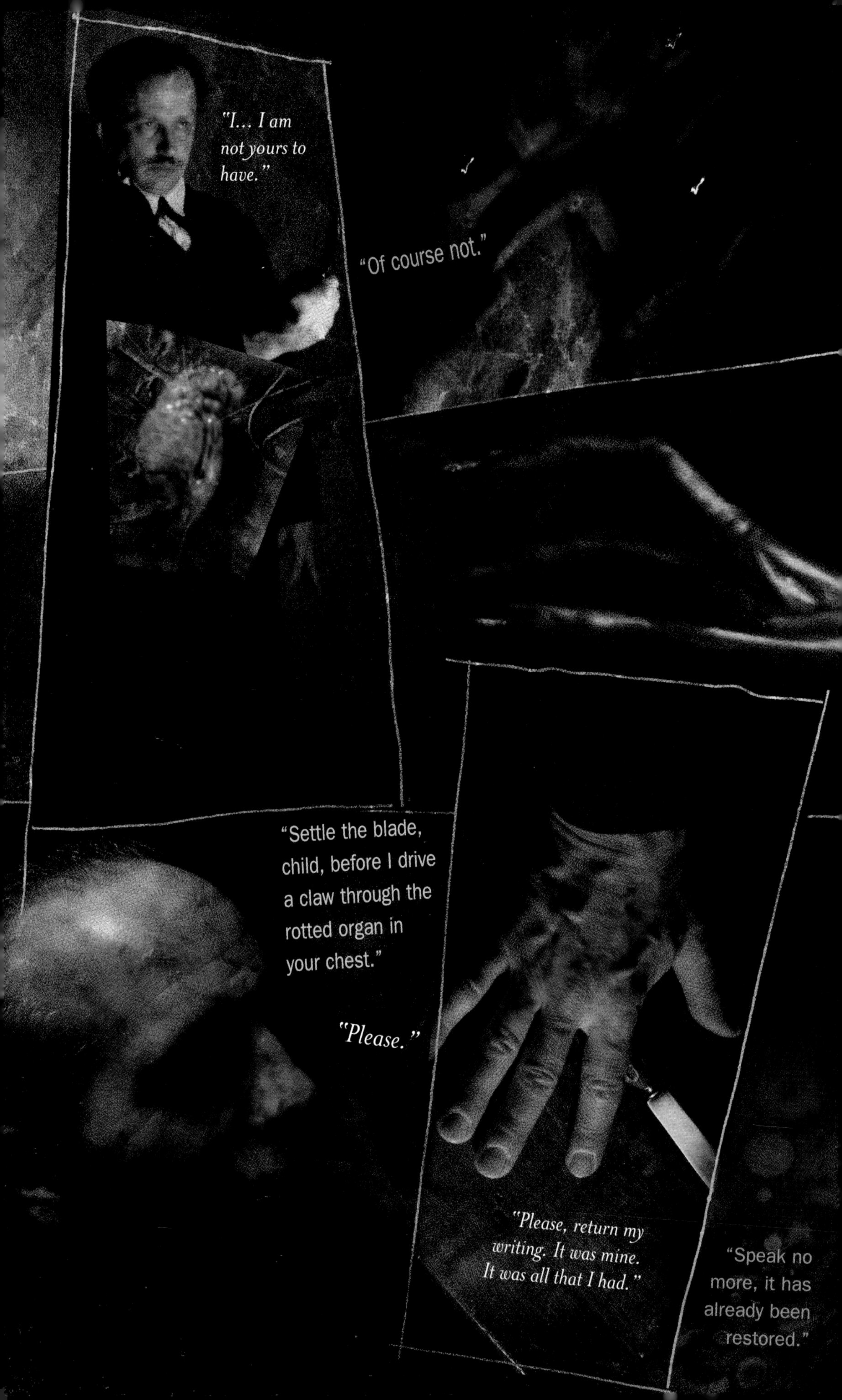
"I... I am not yours to have."
"Of course not."
"Settle the blade, child, before I drive a claw through the rotted organ in your chest."
"Please."
"Please, return my writing. It was mine. It was all that I had."
"Speak no more, it has already been restored."

IN THE FILTHY DAYS that followed, I worked as never before, weaving horrifying stories that illustrated the mockery of my life, both past and present. In that room, whores doing their dirty work above and below, fleas seeking blood, I laid bare the inner-world of haunted men, of people seeking revenge, of those doomed to die lonely.

Before five days was through, I had completed an unfinished story called *The Narrative of Arthur Gordon Pym*.

Further, from scratch I penned *The Fall of the House of Usher*, *The Murders in The Rue Morgue*, and other bits of prose and poetry I would, later, publish to great acclaim.

IT WAS A MIRACLE OFFSET by nighttime pilgrimages through the city, dark strolls when I feared not the dark for its potential since its potential had been reached and misery was at hand. On my last night in Baltimore, exhausted and having written for days, the demons fed hard on my confusion.

"Edgar, you think your precious mother was a virtuous lady? A tramp, she was, a whore with a killer's instinct. Murderer of your father."

"You think he disappeared? Eliza poisoned him. She would have murdered you had she not passed. She hated you. Hate was in her heart."

"She fetched dogs to chew your father's bones. They fed on his body, they did, tore his meat with their teeth."

"Cease, or... I would not come back. I would never return."

"But you will, parasite, he who feeds a stray's bottomless hunger."

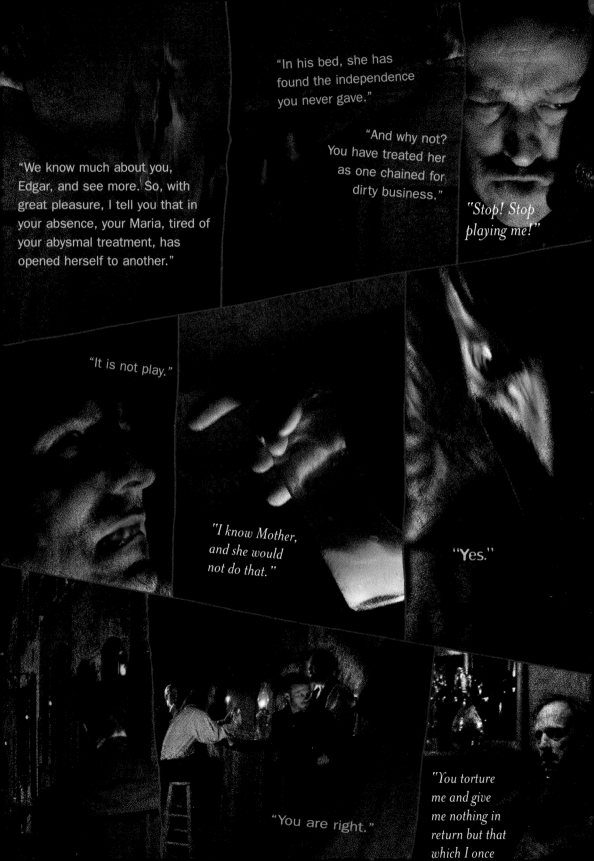

"In his bed, she has found the independence you never gave."

"And why not? You have treated her as one chained for dirty business."

"We know much about you, Edgar, and see more. So, with great pleasure, I tell you that in your absence, your Maria, tired of your abysmal treatment, has opened herself to another."

"Stop! Stop playing me!"

"It is not play."

"I know Mother, and she would not do that."

"Yes."

"You are right."

"You torture me and give me nothing in return but that which I once

"Please, I do not want a joyless life."

"But, of course you will have one. We will see to that."

"Take heart, for you will have great success, Edgar. It sits at your doorsill."

"And yet, by now it must be clear to you that we will deny you

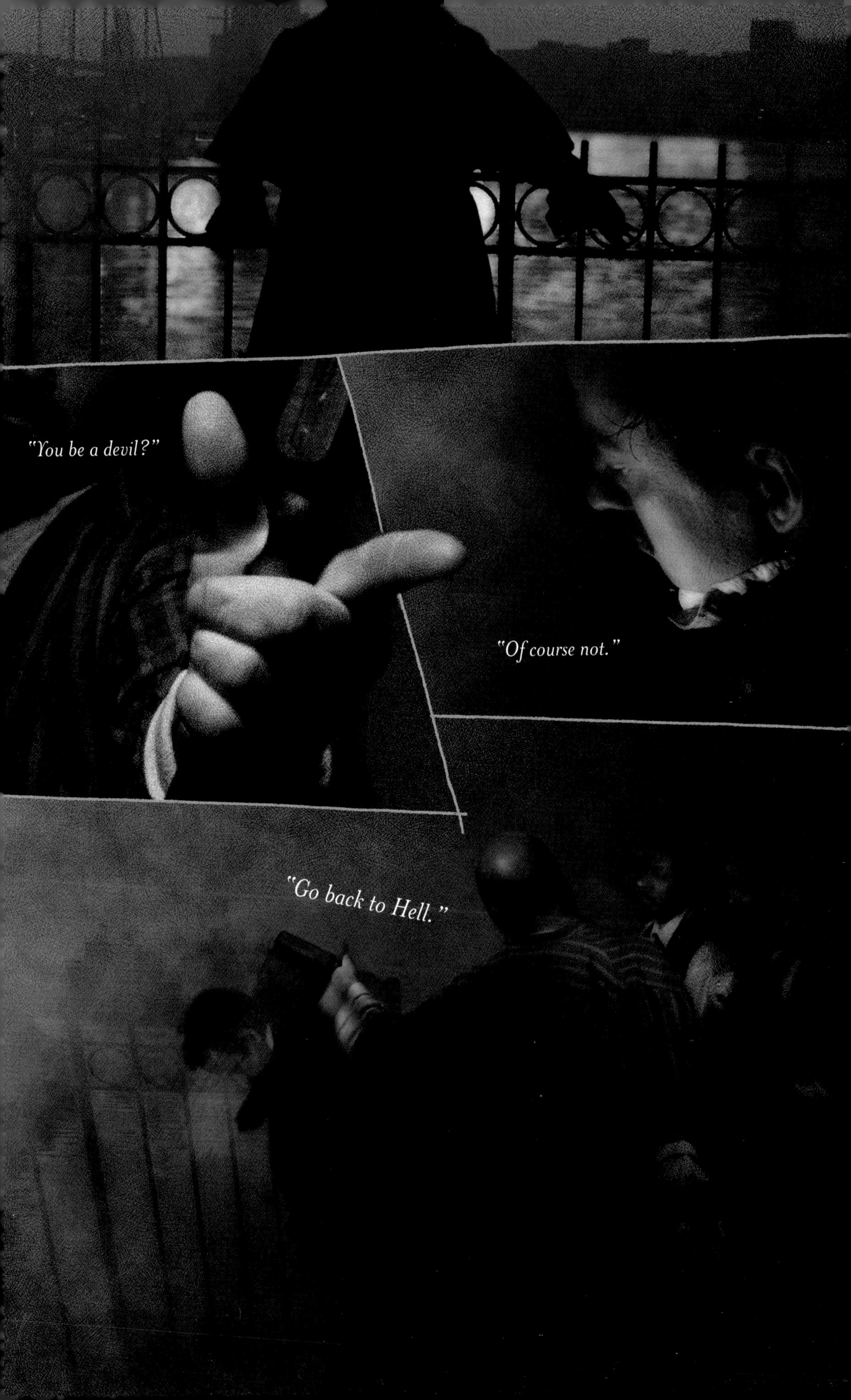
"You be a devil?"
"Of course not."
"Go back to Hell."

On the ground, semi-conscious,
I crawled in search of my balance.

It was through a haze of pain that I
realized my demons would not consent
to my ruination or demise.

Yet, of all possibilities, I would
not have had them save me.

My perceptions were both amplified
and distorted, each vicious sound had an
odd clarity. And, yet, there was one that
rose above others, that pierced the fog...

...that of a demon screeching in pain.

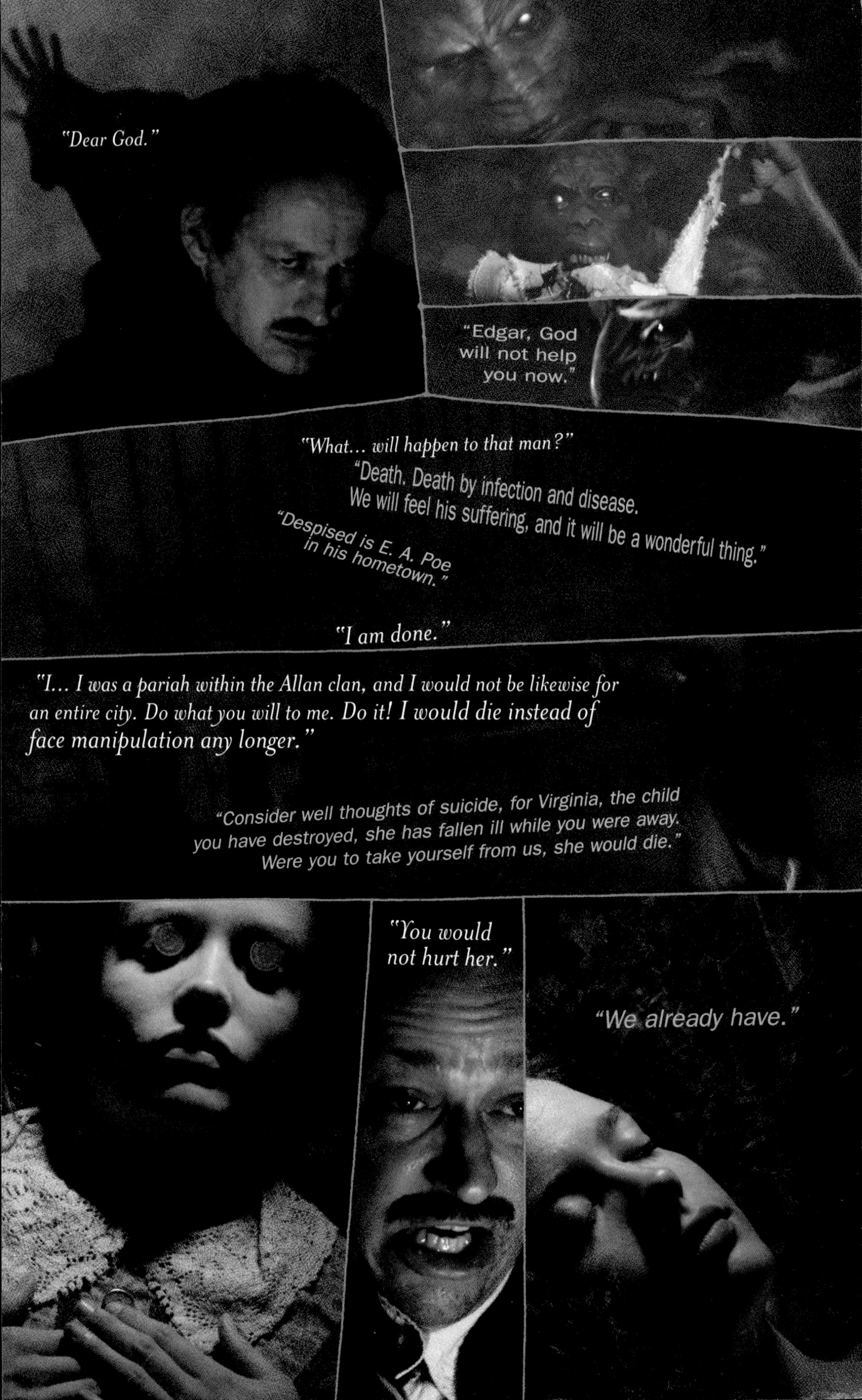
"Dear God."
"Edgar, God will not help you now."
"What... will happen to that man?"
"Death. Death by infection and disease. We will feel his suffering, and it will be a wonderful thing."
"Despised is E. A. Poe in his hometown."
"I am done."
"I... I was a pariah within the Allan clan, and I would not be likewise for an entire city. Do what you will to me. Do it! I would die instead of face manipulation any longer."
"Consider well thoughts of suicide, for Virginia, the child you have destroyed, she has fallen ill while you were away. Were you to take yourself from us, she would die."
"You would not hurt her."
"We already have."

IN DESPERATE SEARCH for eternal life, men have done far worse than I. They have purposefully harmed many. I had not intended to hurt anyone.

I sat with poor Sissy for hours. In her lovely, injured eyes, I saw myself and wished horrible death on my reflection, for her situation was, in actuality, a strike against me.

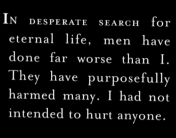

"Eddy?

"I am here to help."

*"In my hurries,
I took a misstep."*

"Your... your head?"

"Eddy? Poor Eddy."

At *The Southern Literary Messenger*, I gained only the smallest satisfaction from publishing new materials and their accompanying accolades. My writing, created in darkness, sickened me.

Regardless, seeking money for Sissy's treatment, I sent away numerous manuscripts, hoping to spark interest and generate an advance.

To my surprise, Harper and Brothers of New York, a most prestigious publisher, responded. It was their intent to purchase *The Narrative of Arthur Gordon Pym,* for they believed it a great work of literature.

I felt only revulsion.

And so began my preordained success, for, after that, magazines and journals across the East sought my work. In all quarters, my writer's reputation was enhanced, my bad habits, for the most part, forgiven.

Speaking offers came by the handful, the pay good if not, at times, generous. Yet, due to the cost of Sissy's treatment, our finances dwindled, so that I remained dependent upon my wretched editorial position.

Then the worst possible outcome occurred. True to his word, Mr. White terminated my besotted employment.

"I am disappointed, Edgar.
I warned you. I begged you.
In… in your heavy consumption,
I should not be at all astonished
to hear that you had been
guilty of suicide."

"You would like to
hear such a thing."

"There, you are
wrong. You are
wrong, Edgar."

"You will live to recall the days of E. A. Poe as the best in The Messenger's history. You have always been ignorant of my talent."

"And what talent might that be? As far as I can tell, you have not penned a word in years. Your success is mere illusion, for I know that you did not write "Pym." I have seen how you root through your handbag of work."

"At your desk, you can barely form proper sentences. Am I to believe you created a masterpiece?"

Stung by Thomas Willis White's words, my confidence hung aslant, like a partially unhinged door. Was my success mere illusion?

Locally, my repute as a drunk was enormous and damning, therefore, no one in the Richmond area would hire me. Thus burned and seeking the best care possible for Sissy, I determined that we should relocate to New York City, a home for great writers and buffoons, men such as myself.

I had small standing in the nation's literary scene and would lean on that to open doors. Further, over so great a distance, word of my poor habits and living arrangements would not follow.

Thus, broke and unhappy I emptied our shabby rooms, and the three of us departed the city of my youth.

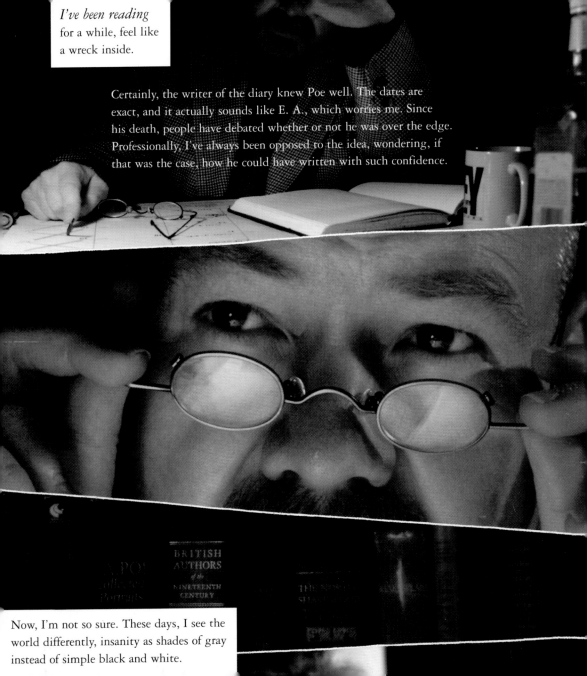

I've been reading for a while, feel like a wreck inside.

Certainly, the writer of the diary knew Poe well. The dates are exact, and it actually sounds like E. A., which worries me. Since his death, people have debated whether or not he was over the edge. Professionally, I've always been opposed to the idea, wondering, if that was the case, how he could have written with such confidence.

Now, I'm not so sure. These days, I see the world differently, insanity as shades of gray instead of simple black and white.

residence in a room on Waverly Place, then, eight months later, for worsening finances, relocated to Carmen Street. Outside of both, frightening men, men who appeared possessed and subjugated to evil, leered at Mother and even sickly Sissy.

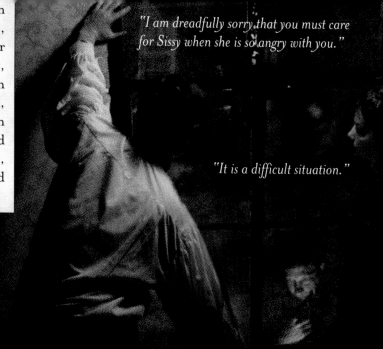

"I am dreadfully sorry that you must care for Sissy when she is so angry with you."

"It is a difficult situation."

"Sissy loves you. I know that. If... if when she is better, we could but change the state of our affairs. Possibly, we could welcome her into our bed. She might improve that much more."

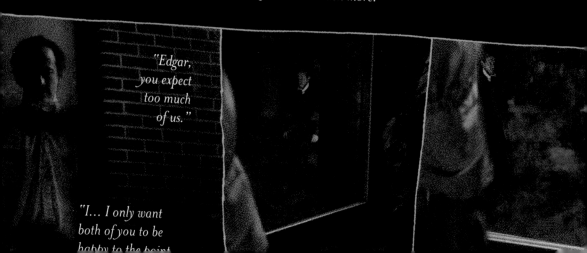

"Edgar, you expect too much of us."

"I... I only want both of you to be happy to the point

Over the next year, and for a handful that followed, our New York lives took a morbid rhythm. As if hauled by chain, I irregularly traveled Southward, where demons set fire my innumerable weaknesses. From those visits, I created notable works, *The Tell-Tale Heart, The Cask of Amontillado, The Premature Burial* and others.

Meanwhile, in New York, doubtlessly managed from afar, contentedness was continually kicked away by untimely events and rumors of my own unseemly, often drunken behavior.

In that way, Sissy's illness nagged, spoiling our finances. However, innocent as she was, whenever she was ambulatory, I hid our distress and stationed myself beside her, sadly privy to her relentless disdain for Mother.

THE TELL-TALE HEART   E.A. POE

"This is all I have ever wanted of you, Eddy, time alone. If we could simply run away, it would be a rebirth."

"It... it is Maria who keeps me ill."

"I beg again, Eddy, if you wish me to improve, do not split time between Maria and myself. That would be a great burden lifted."

"I... I would care ceaselessly for you, but... I could not hurt your mother. I could not."

"Then, Eddy, go to hell. I... I will find someone who would keep me company without hesitation."

"I beg you again, try to understand."

"I cannot."

"I want so much for your happiness. I... I will talk to Mother."

But talk was unnecessary. Strong Maria surrendered me without argument. At night, I loved Sissy whilst I touched Mother as a wife during the day.

AND SO IT WENT, daily, monthly, relentless as a sharpened pendulum blade, our lives forever pulled by unseen strings. Then, from nowhere, the rhythm was suddenly altered. *The Evening Mirror* ran what I believed to be one of my lesser poems, *The Raven*, and our financially burdened past became a separate age from our future.

Evening Mirror.

NEW-YORK, WEDNESDAY, JANUARY 29, 1845.

We are permitted to copy (in advance of publication) from the 2d No. of the American Review, the following remarkable poem by EDGAR POE. In our opinion, it is the most effective single example of "fugitive poetry" ever published in this country; and unsurpassed in English poetry for subtile conception, masterly ingenuity of versification, and consistent, sustaining of imaginative lift and "pokerishness." It is one of these "dainties bred in a book" which we feed on. It will stick to the memory of everybody who reads it.

To me, *The Raven* was a barely veiled metaphor for my existence. It described a man cursed by an indeterminate evil. To my great surprise, however, the public and critics alike perceived deeper notes, and it was their interpretations of *The Raven* that brought me hitherto unattained distinction, placing me amongst the writing elite.

The Raven.

upon a midnight dreary, while I pondered, weak and weary,
many a quaint and curious volume of forgotten lore—
While I nodded, nearly napping, suddenly there came a tapping,
As of some one gently rapping, rapping at my chamber door.
"'Tis some visiter," I muttered, "tapping at my chamber door—
        Only this, and nothing more."

Ah, distinctly I remember it was in the bleak December,
And each separate dying ember wrought its ghost upon the floor.
Eagerly I wished the morrow;—vainly I had tried to borrow
From my books surcease of sorrow—sorrow for the lost Lenore—
For the rare and radiant maiden whom the angels name Lenore—
        Nameless here for evermore.

And the silken sad uncertain rustling of each purple curtain
Thrilled me—filled me with fantastic ter

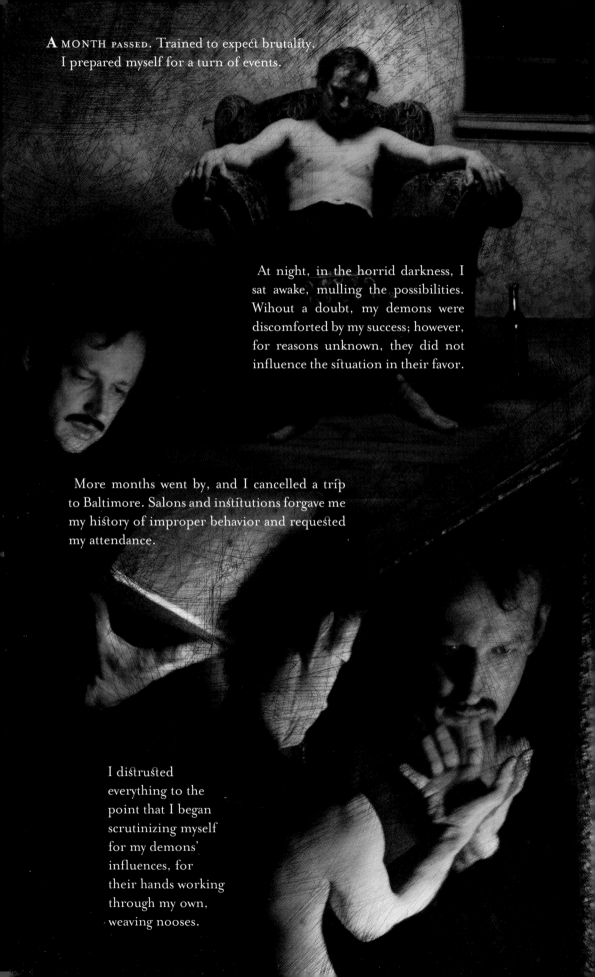

A MONTH PASSED. Trained to expect brutality, I prepared myself for a turn of events.

At night, in the horrid darkness, I sat awake, mulling the possibilities. Wihout a doubt, my demons were discomforted by my success; however, for reasons unknown, they did not influence the situation in their favor.

More months went by, and I cancelled a trip to Baltimore. Salons and institutions forgave me my history of improper behavior and requested my attendance.

I distrusted everything to the point that I began scrutinizing myself for my demons' influences, for their hands working through my own, weaving nooses.

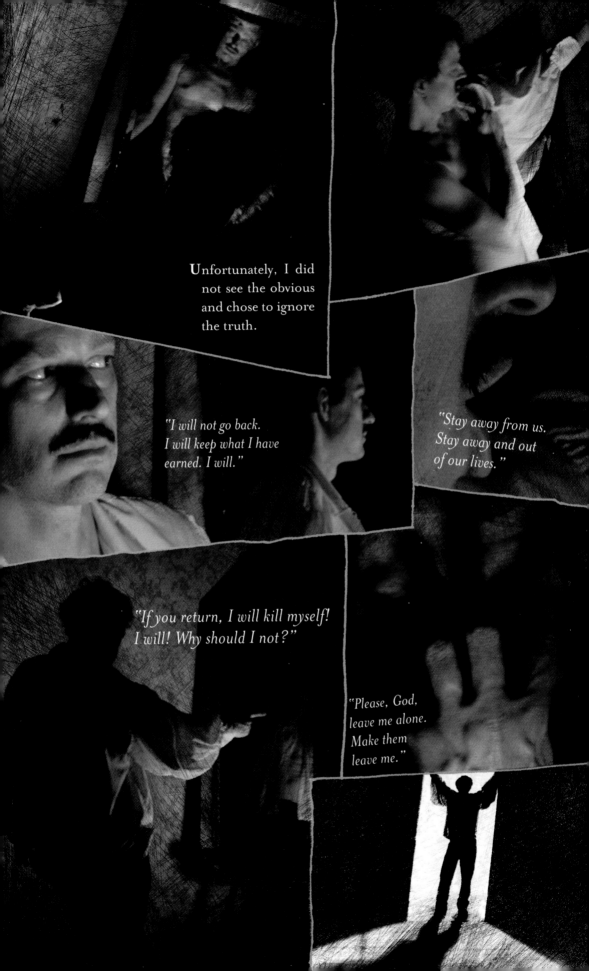

Unfortunately, I did not see the obvious and chose to ignore the truth.

"I will not go back. I will keep what I have earned. I will."

"Stay away from us. Stay away and out of our lives."

"If you return, I will kill myself! I will! Why should I not?"

"Please, God, leave me alone. Make them leave me."

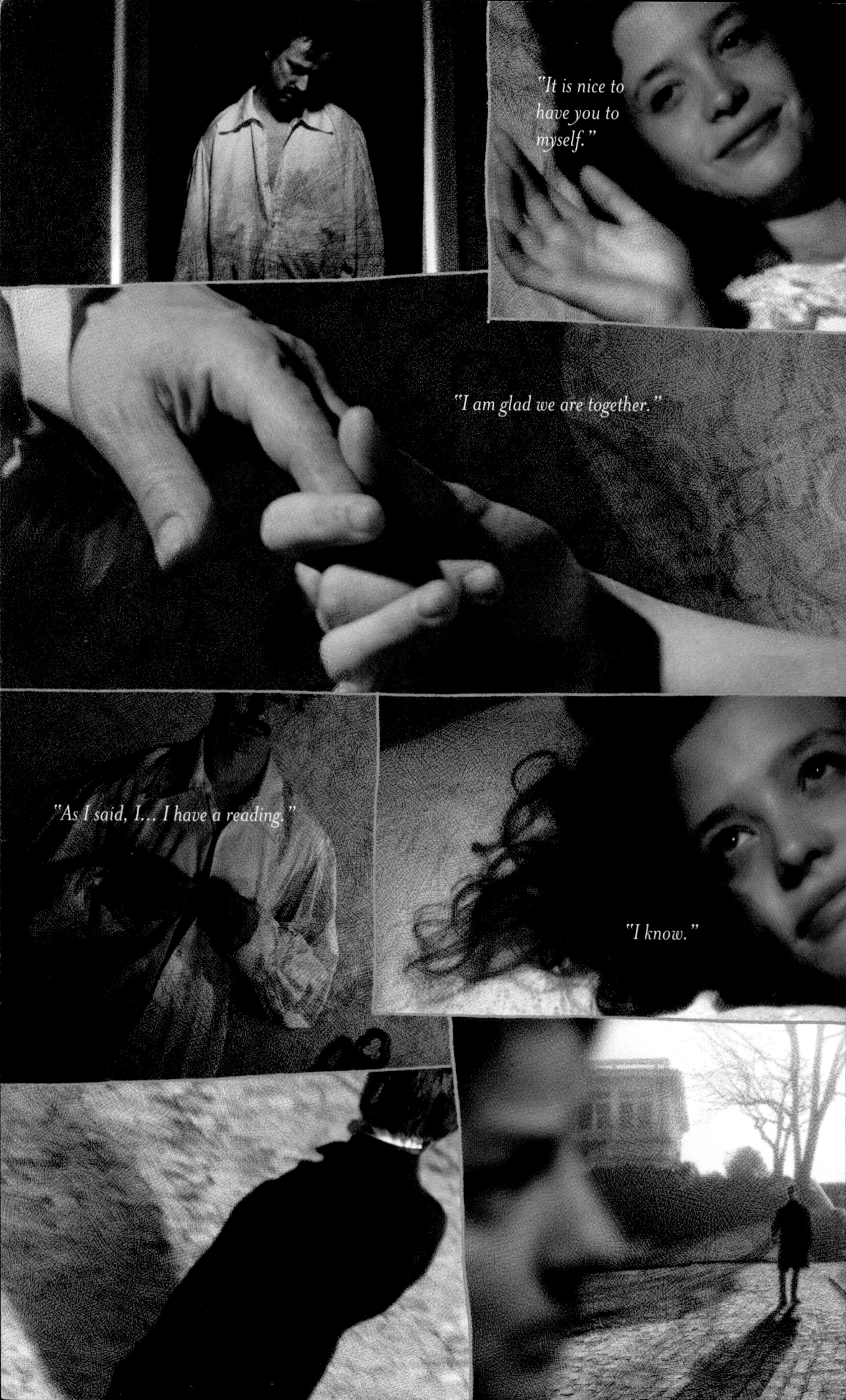
"It is nice to have you to myself."
"I am glad we are together."
"As I said, I... I have a reading."
"I know."

"You were with Sissy?"

"I was,
but, I missed you."

"Take heart, dear Maria,
everything is changing for the
better. Evil has taken flight."

"What evil, Edgar? Your demons were
ever a fabrication of your mind. As you
fear dark shadows after sunset, you fear
dark clouds where none exist."

"Your career has gone well enough.
Have you considered that, more than
anything else, the bottle plagues
you... and us?"

"These days, drink merely helps me
locate a growing sureness. In fact,
right now, I am feeling the early signs
of happiness. I truly am."

"And I... I thank you for that. I thank you for these last six months, for I know it has been difficult on you. But I am only now finding my way free from the past."

"If sleeping with Virginia frees you, I am gladdened. But yes, it has been difficult."

"I would change things soon."

"Edgar, stop. I... I have given you everything at great expense to myself and would beg you to silence. In fact... I... I fear that the distance between us is God's penance for our sins. For we have sinned, this we should acknowl..."

"Mother, He is not angered. God cannot fault us. He knows we must nurture Sissy. In fact, I see now that he may have a hand in this arrangement, for over the years we have not responded in a form they foresaw."

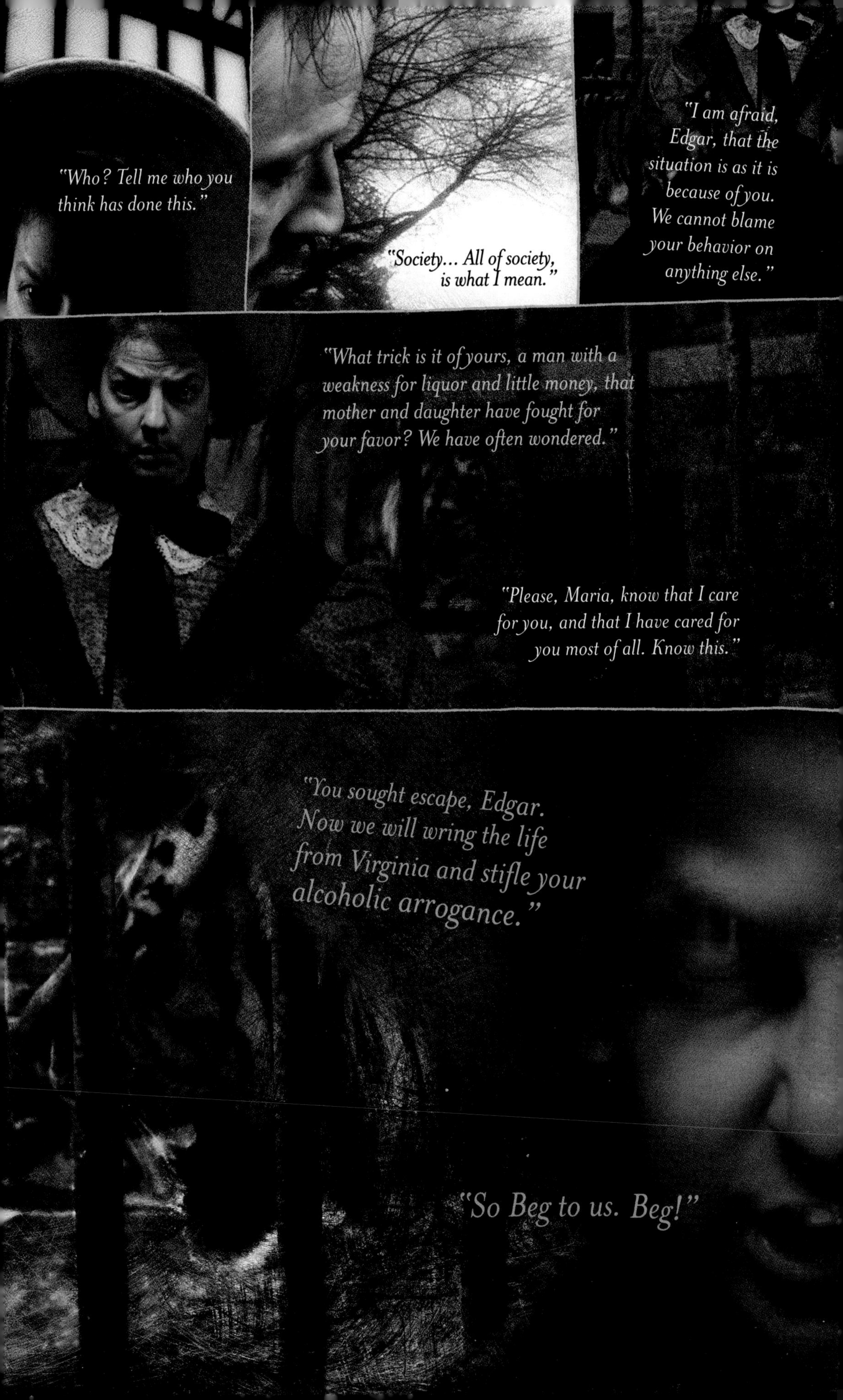
"Who? Tell me who you think has done this."
"Society... All of society, is what I mean."
"I am afraid, Edgar, that the situation is as it is because of you. We cannot blame your behavior on anything else."
"What trick is it of yours, a man with a weakness for liquor and little money, that mother and daughter have fought for your favor? We have often wondered."
"Please, Maria, know that I care for you, and that I have cared for you most of all. Know this."
"You sought escape, Edgar. Now we will wring the life from Virginia and stifle your alcoholic arrogance."
"So Beg to us. Beg!"

"Mother?"

"Mother, what say you?
Dear God, what say you?"

"I... I have said nothing."

"No. No, you spoke cruel words."

"Edgar, what has frightened you?"

"You... you threatened to murder Sissy."

"How... how could you say such a thing?"

"Edgar?"

"Sissy, I love you. I do. Don't worry.
I... I have been awaiting this moment,
that is all. That is all. Now, go inside.
Flee the cold. Please."

WITH HARROWING SWIFTNESS, her fitful health took a devastating turn for the worse.

"It… it is my fault. Love, it is my fault. I am to blame. If I had been braver, this… this would not be. You are innocent in my affairs."

"You should know, Eddy, I am not truly sick. Maria is poisoning me. Do you see? Do not allow her into our room. She administers toxins."

"She despises me."

"No, it is something else."

"Sissy, I wish it were me. It should be me."

"Take me!"

"Yer going ta upset her, sir. Let her be. Let her pass in peace."

So, by manner of acute grief, small honor surfaced in me. For it was in the aftermath of Sissy's passing that I recognized a singular obligation: In order to keep Mother safe, I needed to remove myself from her.

"Mother, I am not the man I was. I... I think of what I didn't give and what I have caused, and a great pall covers me. I am devastated by loss."

"Edgar, be strong. Possibly, it is better this way."

"But, I am to blame. You do not know. So, yes, I need be strong and honest."

"Mother, I say as clearly as I can, I no longer love you. Now that we have lost Sissy, there is nothing left for us. We were three, not two."

"Edgar, stop. You are simply taxed by Sissy's burial. I..."

"I speak truth."

"Please, Edgar. Quiet yourself. Let us return home together. Don't you see, I... I have freed us. I have..."

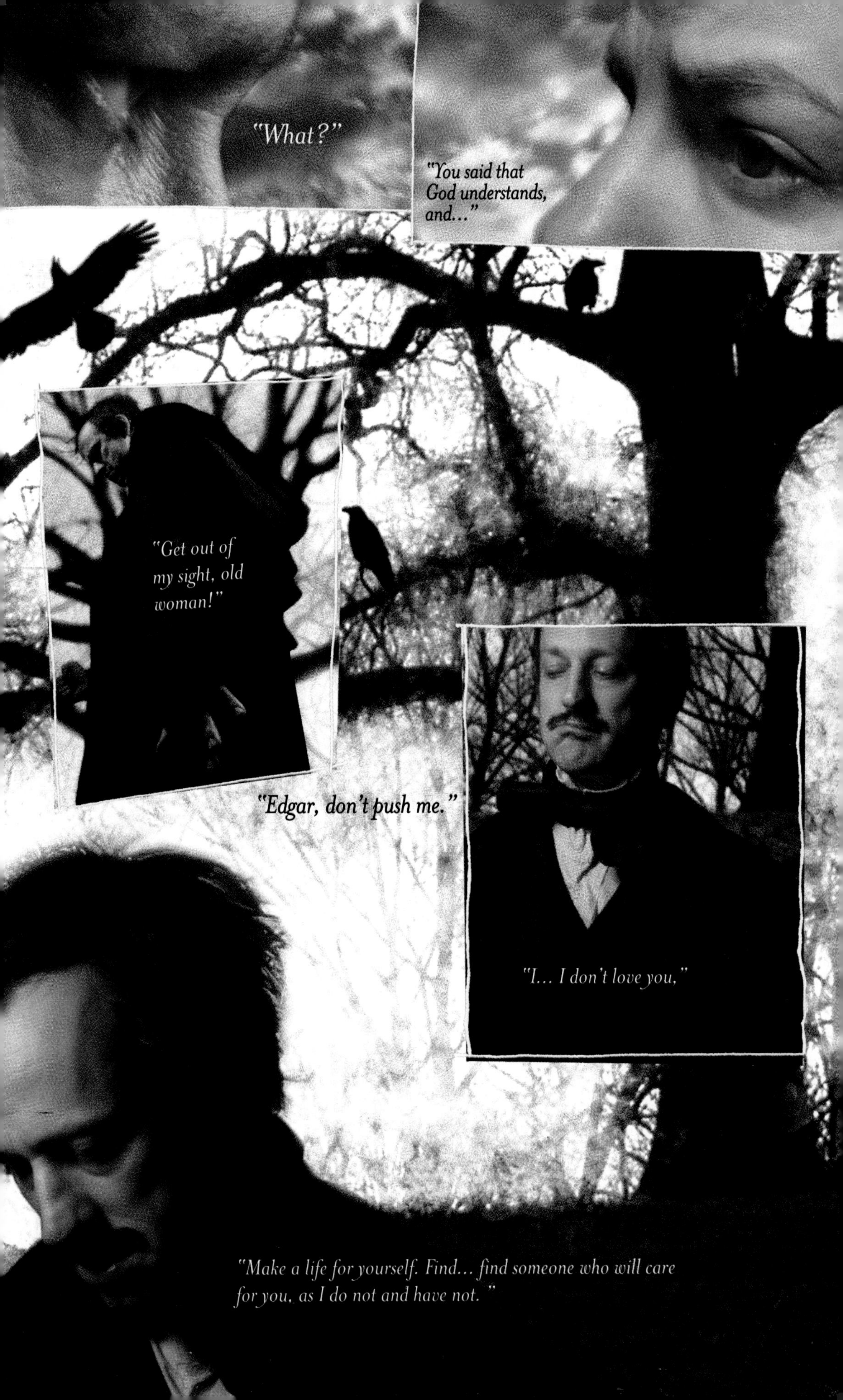
"What?"
"You said that God understands, and..."
"Get out of my sight, old woman!"
"Edgar, don't push me."
"I... I don't love you."
"Make a life for yourself. Find... find someone who will care for you, as I do not and have not."

"Step anew into the world, Mother."

"Understand that your sins are mine own."

Like a boat set free in rushing water, I had no harbor and no home. Spiritually shattered, I was left bereft of all but two cold and unadorned desires. I wanted to protect Mother and gain small retribution.

THAT NIGHT, and for the few that remained, my grinding teeth and growing rage kept me company. Had they so corrupted Mother that she actually murdered Sissy? I could not believe. Mother was surely innocent.

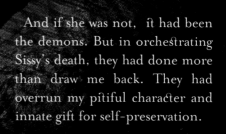

And if she was not, it had been the demons. But in orchestrating Sissy's death, they had done more than draw me back. They had overrun my pitiful character and innate gift for self-preservation.

I ARRIVED IN BALTIMORE in the late afternoon, where I wandered the streets, sober and, for once, gladly anticipating the darkness of nighttime.

I did not know if my demons could die, but I had seen them injured and would take pleasure in seeing similar again. I would inflict pain and force them to kill me in return, for I was sure that my death would hurt them most. As for me, dying was an outcome preferable to living. I despised myself for the pain I had brought to Sissy and Mother.

"We have taught you a lesson, Edgar. You will not dismiss us."

"I seek physical evidence, so that people can see of what I write."

"Where go we?"

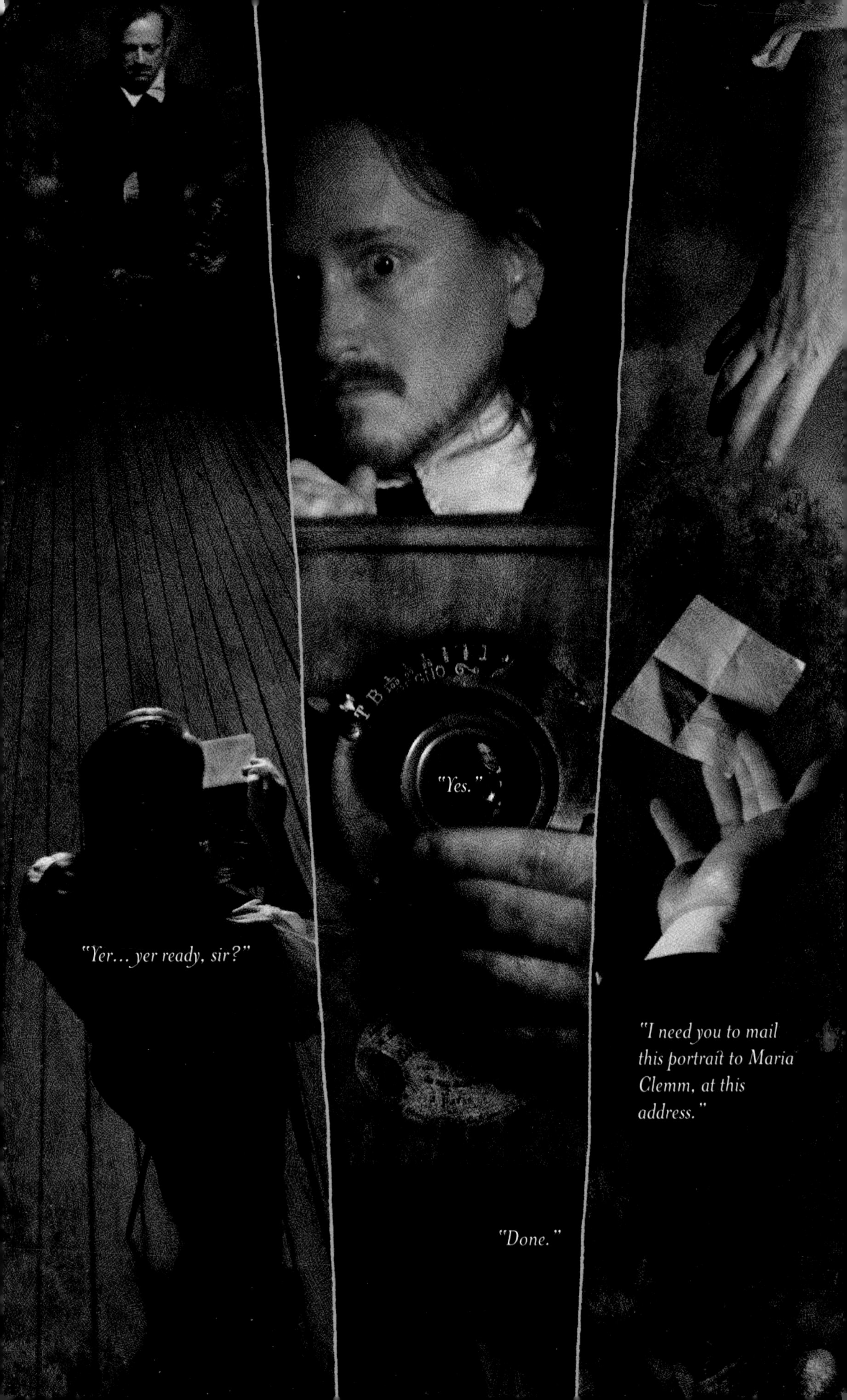
"Yer... yer ready, sir?"
"Yes."
"I need you to mail this portrait to Maria Clemm, at this address."
"Done."

"I see now that, in the name of your niece, you would wade into us, Edgar. Is that your thought? We who have witnessed empires of the Old World fall.

"We who have watched generations pass by age, plague, and war."

"We have known spineless men such as you. We have dealt wih your kind. You are too weak to attain revenge. "

"You are no different from Dante and Michelangelo and Bosch. A man as you lived in Rome and moved his empire to Constantinople seeking escape."

"We are sustained by broken brilliance. We know our way and means, as a lion knows how to disembowel."

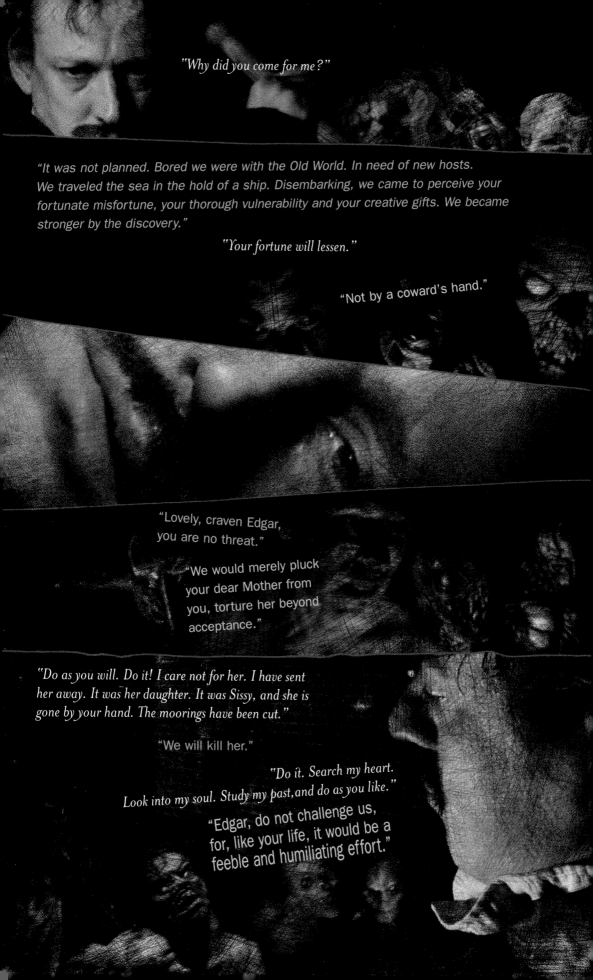

"Why did you come for me?"

"It was not planned. Bored we were with the Old World. In need of new hosts. We traveled the sea in the hold of a ship. Disembarking, we came to perceive your fortunate misfortune, your thorough vulnerability and your creative gifts. We became stronger by the discovery."

"Your fortune will lessen."

"Not by a coward's hand."

"Lovely, craven Edgar, you are no threat."

"We would merely pluck your dear Mother from you, torture her beyond acceptance."

"Do as you will. Do it! I care not for her. I have sent her away. It was her daughter. It was Sissy, and she is gone by your hand. The moorings have been cut."

"We will kill her."

"Do it. Search my heart. Look into my soul. Study my past, and do as you like."

"Edgar, do not challenge us, for, like your life, it would be a feeble and humiliating effort."

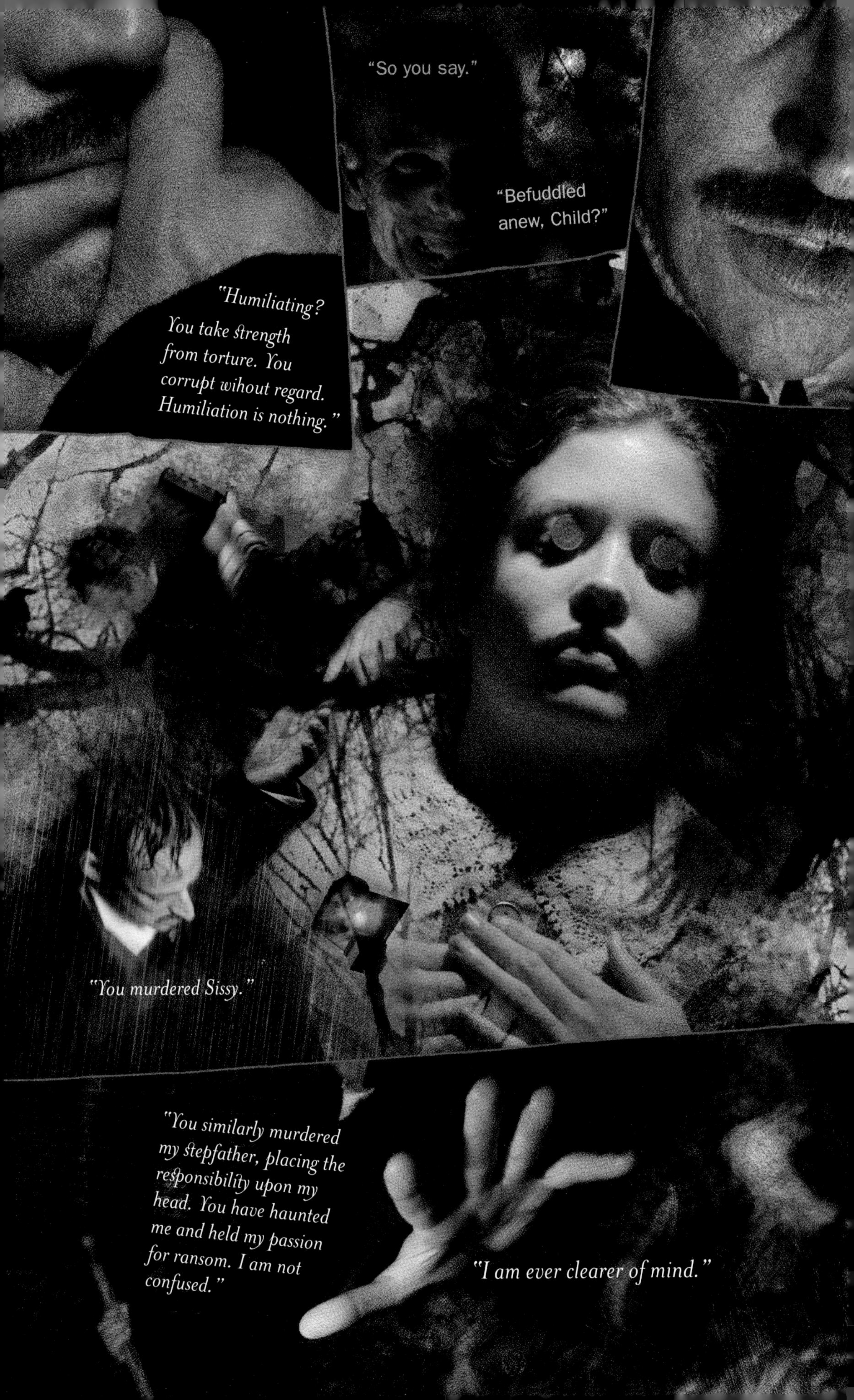
"So you say."
"Befuddled anew, Child?"
"Humiliating? You take strength from torture. You corrupt wihout regard. Humiliation is nothing."
"You murdered Sissy."
"You similarly murdered my stepfather, placing the responsibility upon my head. You have haunted me and held my passion for ransom. I am not confused."
"I am ever clearer of mind."

"But, you miscalculate, Edgar. We have done nothing, and that is the beauty. It was your own weaknesses that invested us with powers we do not possess."

"We claimed reponsibility for preordained events, as meager fortune-tellers are wont to do."

"Your writing was always available to you. It was your own fragile wits that surrendered it. You believed you could not write, and that was enough."

"You are liars!"

"Regain yourself, Edgar. There are endless forms of torture, even from the grave."

"So you say I have misunderstood?"

"It was not you who maintained the cruel details of my life, but myself and mere misfortune?"

"We have done nothing."

"You controlled everything."

"You misunderstood, that is all."

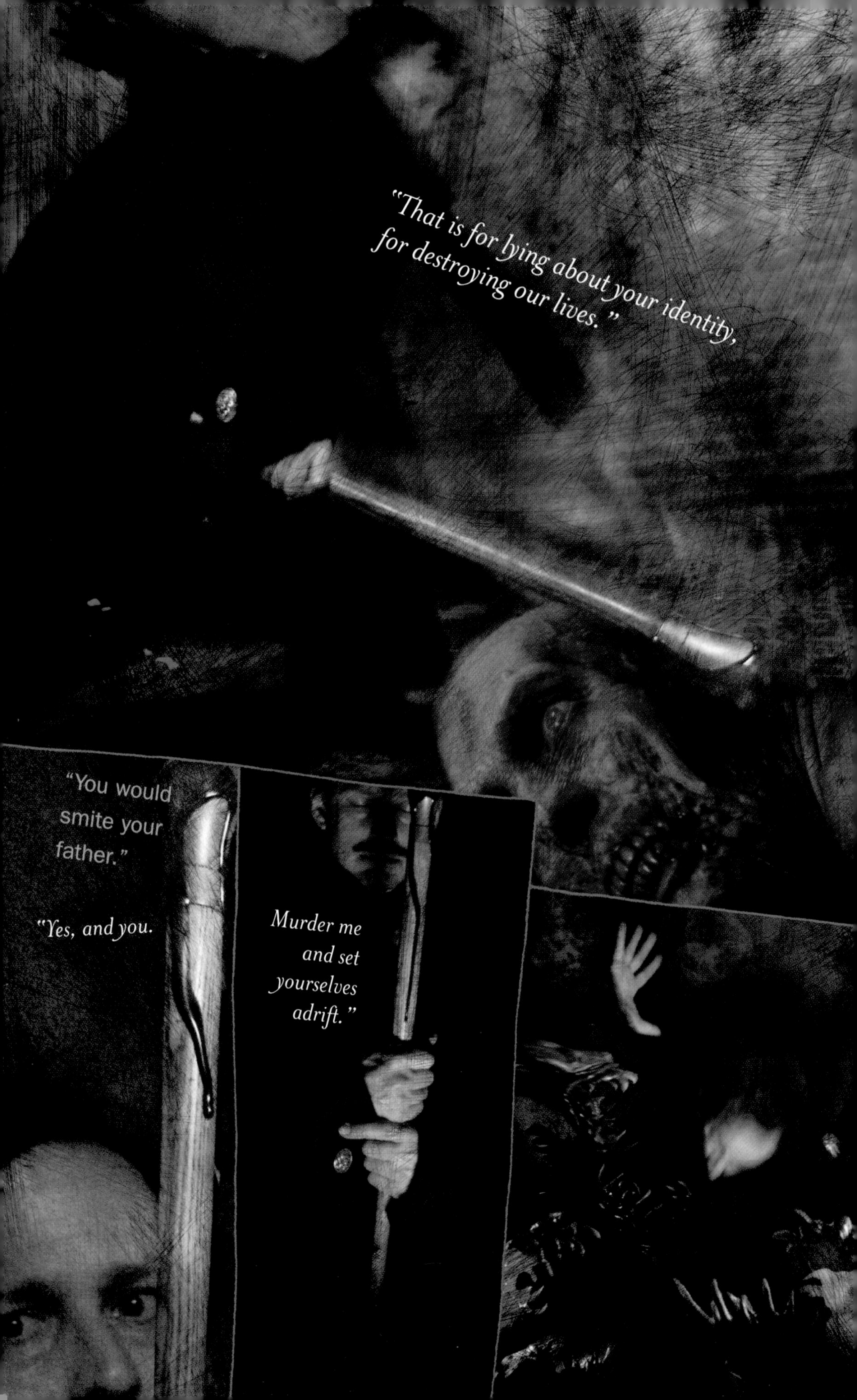
"That is for lying about your identity, for destroying our lives."
"You would smite your father."
"Yes, and you.
Murder me and set yourselves adrift."

A FEVER RISES in wounds that only I can see. I beg God to
treat my loved ones well, especially Mother, whom I have
cared for with all my heart. We may have engaged in a lifetime of sinful acts, but we have adored one another and,
no matter the truth, dear Sissy, too.

As horrible as I am, I have always
cared for them more than myself,
for, in sending Mother away, in
committing the most painful act of
my life, I hoped to save her.

Now I seek cold truth and my other demon, drink, to ease the
pain. I am sober and end my confessional with a temperate plea.
Despite those things with which I have conspired, I beg for
salvation and freedom from evils.

Forgive me.

It is a known fact that Poe was found "in great distress," drunken in a bar. Sick and bedraggled, the writer was carted off to Washington Medical College and dumped in a section reserved for drunks.

In the few days that Poe was there, he fluctuated in and out of delirium. The doctor working his case tried cheering him by saying that he would soon recover and return to the company of his friends. Poe's response was chilling.

"The best thing any friend can do is blow my brains out wih a pistol."

Early on Ocober 7, 1849, Poe began calling out indecipherable names. A few hours later, a doctor reported that he began to move his head back and forth before finally shouting, "Lord help my poor soul!" Then he died.

Reportedly, the final image of Poe was taken in Richmond, but if he sent it from Baltimore, the provenance might have gotten confused.

After her death, I had long discussions with my wife.

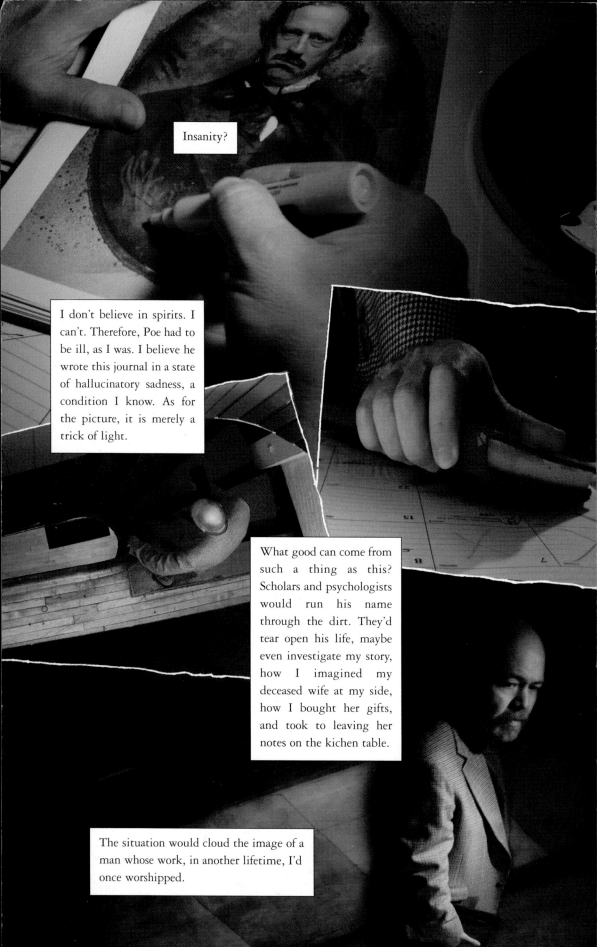

Insanity?

I don't believe in spirits. I can't. Therefore, Poe had to be ill, as I was. I believe he wrote this journal in a state of hallucinatory sadness, a condition I know. As for the picture, it is merely a trick of light.

What good can come from such a thing as this? Scholars and psychologists would run his name through the dirt. They'd tear open his life, maybe even investigate my story, how I imagined my deceased wife at my side, how I bought her gifts, and took to leaving her notes on the kichen table.

The situation would cloud the image of a man whose work, in another lifetime, I'd once worshipped.

And no wonder my friend didn't trust me with what he believed to be a forgery of little value. I'm unpredictable these days. I would destroy things that don't belong to me even as I began destroying myself. But, it seems that while one type of destruction can be partially undone, I would make sure that the other was permanent.

I expunge Poe's diary from the record, save both of us from trespassers. I can only imagine the effect of so much loss on a mind, and, to the extent that I can, I sympathize.

Loss takes away the edges, leaves nothing but ghosts… and demons.

Storyboarded by Jonathon and Steve   *Storyboard art by Farel Dalrymple*

SUPPORTING CAST: *Thomas Willis White—Jeffrey Pratt Gordon*
John Allan—Michael Northrup; Father Demon—Duane Herbel; One-Armed Man—Thomas Rhodes

EXTRAS: *Calla Fuqua, George Goebel, Julie Lauffenberger, Kathryn Parke,*
Ethan McGann Phillips, Gwendolyn McGann Phillips, Shawn Colin Phillips,
E. Rachel Baird, Dan Buccino, Scott Larsen, Tim Nelson, Kevin Perkins, Darius Scott

DEMON FIGURES PROVIDED/SCULPTED BY:
William Paquet—Paquet Figure Works, Casey Love—theCloneFactory,
Mike Elizalde—Spectral Motion, Bob Baggy—Jeff Taylor Designs, Dave Britton, Richard Leach
Demons built and painted by Steve except father Demon—painted by David Fisher

SPECIAL THANKS To:
A. T. Jones Costumers of Baltimore, Adobe Systems, A-1 Taxidermy of Baltimore, Amazing
Figure Modeler, Terri Anderson, Andromeda Software—Etchtone and Scatterlight filters,
Dragonwing Studios, E.A. Poe Society, Harriet at Artistic Dance and Costumes, John Fell
House; Key Coffee Roasters, Killerfonts.com—Poe handwriting, Service Photo, Lara
Vacante, Terry Webb, Ship model handmade by Charles R. Probst Sr. courtesy Mike Probst.

Typeset in part with the Mrs. Eaves font family designed by Zuzana Licko in 1996 for Émigré.

EXTRA THANKS TO THE CITY OF BALTIMORE:
for the preservation of its neighborhoods
and architecture so a project like this could be undertaken.

SCOTT'S THANKS:
First, I need to thank Steve Parke for having thirty ideas a minute and allowing me
to filter through a few of them. Steve is a brilliant, hilarious man and a wonderful
friend. Of course, I thank my wife and daughter, both of whom I love dearly. Thanks
also go to my loving and brilliant extended family. I give the nod to Steven John
Phillips for his graciousness, cool attitude, and eye. As for my own creative demons,
I don't think the little bastards deserve a thanks since they've done more harm than
good. Thank you Sue Mangan for your sharp comments, kind words, and unique
vision (also and unfortunately, I should add, haunted by demons). Thanks to all the
gifted actors, especially Damon, who pulled off my vision with amazing clarity.
Thanks Robbie. Thanks Candlewick for being such a cool publisher. I hope everybody
enjoys the book.

STEVE'S THANKS
Foremost I'd like to thank Scott and Stephen for being easy to work with; talent
rarely lacks so much ego. I am grateful these two people are my friends; without them
this idea would have remained just that. My lovely wife for letting me come home late
and making sure I didn't eat Pop Tarts all day, and my son for still recognizing me as
"daddy." My late cat Miko's ghost who greeted me at the gate like old times after a
long night of work. Susan for continuing to smack me in the head when I needed it and
her way with a font. All the sculptors who lent their talent, especially the brilliant
William Paquet for his original Raven design sculpted for this project. Lastly, the
unbelievable actors and non actors who breathed life into these characters.

STEPHEN'S THANKS
Our heartfelt thanks to George, Rick, & Mary and the staff of A. T. Jones Costumers
of Baltimore for once again providing the fantastic wardrobe. A world-class costumer
who takes time and pity on our projects. To Abe & Chuck who guided us through the
myriad of digital options on the market and to Burke for having the sense to hire them.
Ann Mckim Gordon Phillips for understanding, support and letting me off the hook at
school events.